CULTURES OF THE WORLD
Tunisia

Cavendish
Square

New York

Published in 2018 by Cavendish Square Publishing, LLC
243 5th Avenue, Suite 136, New York, NY 10016
Copyright © 2018 by Cavendish Square Publishing, LLC

Third Edition

Library of Congress Cataloging-in-Publication Data

Names: Brown, Roslind Varghese, author. | Spilling, Michael, author. |
   Nevins, Debbie, author.
Title: Tunisia / Rosalind Varghese Brown, Michael Spilling, Debbie Nevins.
Description: Third edition. | New York : Cavendish Square Publishing, 2018. |
   Series: Cultures of the world (Third edition) | Includes bibliographical
   references and index.
Identifiers: LCCN 2017034825 (print) | LCCN 2017035882 (ebook) | ISBN
   9781502632364 (e-book) | ISBN 9781502632357 (library bound : alk. paper)
Subjects: LCSH: Tunisia--Juvenile literature.
Classification: LCC DT245 (ebook) | LCC DT245 .B76 2017 (print) | DDC
   961.1--dc23
LC record available at https://lccn.loc.gov/2017034825

Writers, Rosalind Varghese Brown, Michael Spilling; Debbie Nevins, third edition
Editorial Director, third edition: David McNamara
Editor, third edition: Debbie Nevins
Art Director, third edition: Amy Greenan
Designer, third edition: Jessica Nevins
Picture Researcher, third edition: Jessica Nevins

PICTURE CREDITS

PRECEDING PAGE
A view of the ruins of ancient Carthage and the Gulf of Tunis beyond, as seen from Byrsa Hill.

Printed in the United States of America

CONTENTS

TUNISIA TODAY

TUNISIA IS A COUNTRY ON THE MEDITERRANEAN COAST OF Africa. Like its North African neighbors from Morocco in the west to Egypt in the east, it is an Arab nation rooted in Islam, and the religion is a strong influence on its culture. Home to the ancient city of Carthage and close to vital shipping routes, Tunisia has long been an important player in Mediterranean affairs. Romans, Arabs, Ottoman Turks, and French colonialists have all ruled the country at different times, leaving behind their influences, which are still apparent today.

In terms of recent history, Tunisia has the distinction of being the place where the "Arab Spring" uprisings began in 2010—2011. Following Tunisia's brief but violent revolution, which ousted a longtime dictator, a wave of pro-democracy rebellions swept across Arab nations, with largely unsuccessful results. In the aftermath, Tunisia itself is still in transition. It's the only one of the Arab countries to emerge from the upheaval with a new constitution, more civil liberties and political freedoms, and a more representative form of government.

But Tunisia's fledgling democracy is not out of the woods yet by any means. Many challenges remain, including poverty and dire economic conditions, corruption, and

Tunisians weep after police killed a young protester in the town of Thala on January 12, 2011. Two days later, President Ben Ali would flee the country.

terrorism. Young people, in particular, suffer from a lack of opportunity. In despair, increasing numbers have followed the example of Mohamed Bouazizi, the Tunisian street vendor whose self-immolation—a public act of protest—set off the Tunisian Revolution in December 2010. In the five years following the revolution, cases of self-immolation tripled in Tunisia. In 2016, the country's main burn hospital in Ben Arous, a suburb of Tunis, admitted a record 104 patients, mostly young men, who had set fire to themselves.

Thousands of other young men have left home to join the Islamic State (ISIS), the militant fundamentalist group that has swept the Arab world. ISIS thrives in failed states, and has risen up in Syria, Iraq, Libya, and other war-torn regions. In fact, more of the group's jihadist fighters have come from Tunisia than from any other country. One unforeseen and unintended consequence of the pro-democracy Tunisian revolt has been the rise of militant fundamentalist Islamist groups. Under the previous authoritarian government, Islamist groups were suppressed, and even brutally oppressed. Now their influence is being felt in small but significant ways.

For example, in June 2017, four men were sentenced to one month in prison for eating and smoking in public during Ramadan, Islam's holy month. (During Ramadan, Muslims fast during daylight hours.) The court in Bizerte, a city in northern Tunisia, determined the men's activities to be a "provocative act." Although the new 2014 constitution designates the state as the "guardian of religion"—and devout Muslims might well find the four men's public eating to be deeply offensive—it also protects religious freedom. Tunisia has no law against eating in public during Ramadan, but the men were still convicted.

In a similar case, in April 2017, a British DJ called Dax J was sentenced in Tunisia to one year in jail, charged with public indecency and offending public morality. The London-born DJ had performed at a festival in Nabeul, in

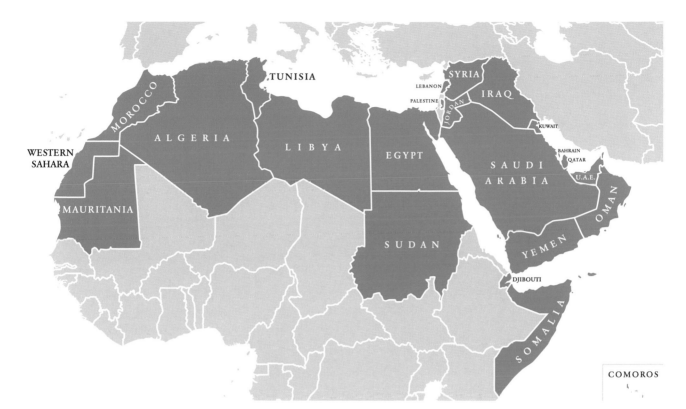

northeastern Tunisia, playing music that included a dance remix of a Muslim call to prayer. The governor of Nabeul, Mnaouar Ouertani, said, "We will not allow attacks against religious feelings and the sacred." Dax J had already left the country prior to the court decision, and had issued an apology. Nevertheless, he received death threats.

The militant Islamist influence is being felt in other ways as well. In 2013, two popular leftist politicians were assassinated by radical Islamist militants. The victims had opposed Islamist elements in Tunisian politics. In 2015, two terrorist attacks occurred at two of Tunisia's major tourist destinations. In the first, gunmen targeted foreigners visiting the famous Bardo Museum in Tunis, killing twenty-one people and injuring forty-seven others. A couple of months later, a lone gunman killed thirty-eight tourists on a beach in Sousse.

Tourism is vital to Tunisia's economy. With its long Mediterranean coastline and beautiful sand beaches, it attracts Europeans seeking warm, sunny resorts. After the terror attacks, a number of countries, including the

Tunisia is part of the Arab world. It's one of the twenty-two Arabic-speaking countries (shown here in green) that make up the Arab League, an organization for cooperation between these nations. (Syria's participation was suspended in 2011 in response to the government's repressive actions during the Syrian Civil War.)

United Kingdom, issued advisories against travel to Tunisia. Naturally, the country's tourism numbers dropped precipitously. This in turn hurt many thousands of average Tunisians who earn their livings catering to tourists. The militants' objective is to destabilize the government so that a fundamentalist caliphate, or Islamist state, can take hold.

Though a majority of Tunisians prefer to see their country lean toward democracy, high unemployment rates continue to embitter and frustrate many people. This trend plays into a vicious circle—disaffected young people call for revolution, which destabilizes society, which scares off the foreign investors who would finance new business endeavors and improve job prospects. The unhealthy economy breeds corruption, which then undermines people's faith in their government, and on it goes.

In June 2017, however, Prime Minister Youssef Chahed earned the respect of many of his countrymen. He led a sweeping crackdown on corruption, which is seen as one of the greatest threats to Tunisia's new democracy. Corruption in public contracting alone is reportedly costing the country

nearly $1 billion a year. Under Chahed's direction, a host of organized crime leaders were arrested, with promises of many more to come. Among the greatest of the corrupt officials and bureaucrats are the former president Zine el-Abidine Ben Ali, who was ousted by the Tunisian Revolution of 2011, and his extended family. Ben Ali resides now in Saudi Arabia, beyond the scope of Chahed's reach.

The prime minister's operation is just one of numerous optimistic signs that Tunisia might actually succeed as a relatively free Muslim nation. If it does, it will be in a position to lead North Africa and the Arab world ahead to peace, prosperity, and modernity. Tunisia is a fairly small country, and those are mighty objectives, but the Tunisian people continue to hold out hope.

On July 20, 2017, Tunisian Prime Minister Youssef Chahed addresses the parliament on the country's fight against corruption.

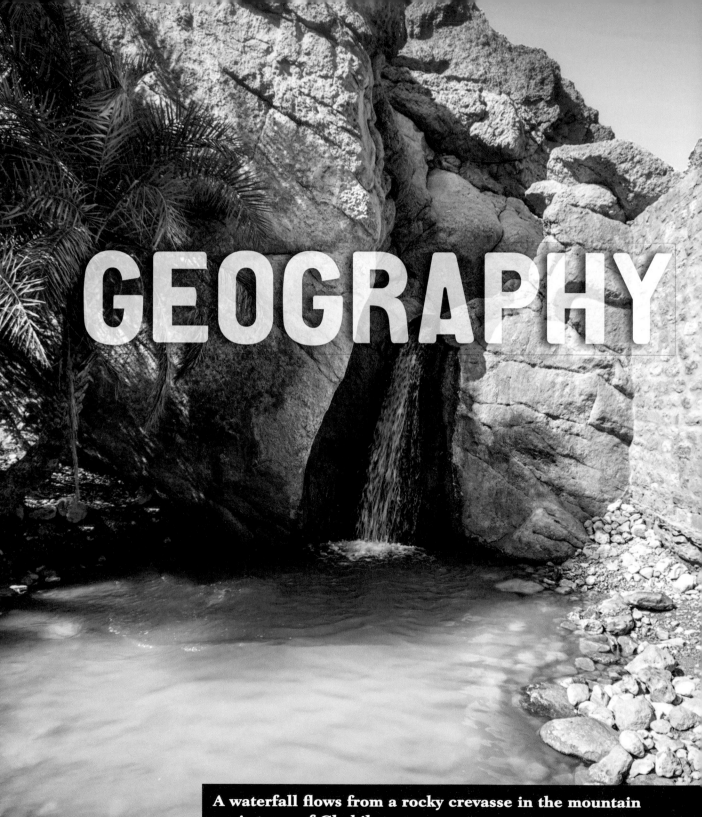

GEOGRAPHY

A waterfall flows from a rocky crevasse in the mountain oasis town of Chebika.

1

TUNISIA IS THE SMALLEST COUNTRY in North Africa—that is, the continental expanse between the Sahara Desert and Mediterranean Sea. Located on the northernmost tip of Africa, on the Mediterranean coast, it is a wedge of land between Algeria and Libya.

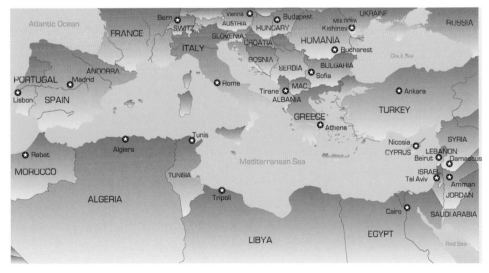

This map shows Tunisia and the other countries that surround the Mediterranean Sea.

After the Arabs conquered North Africa in the seventh century, they called the territory under their control the Maghreb (or Maghrib), meaning "the Arab West." The term is still used today, and includes Morocco, Algeria, Tunisia at its core, and sometimes Libya and Mauritania. The cultures, religions, languages, and cuisines of the Maghreb are similar, though each country has its own individuality.

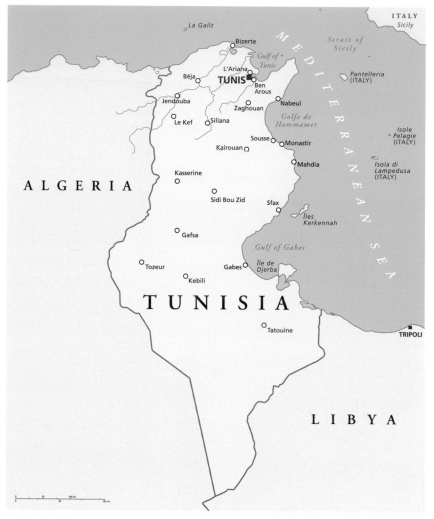

Most of Tunisia's population centers are in the north.

Tunisia has a land area of 63,170 square miles (163,610 sq kilometers), approximately the size of the state of Missouri. It's slightly smaller than the state of Florida, or of England and Wales combined. Nearly half of its total boundary is coastline. Tunis, the capital, lies on its northern coast.

Aside from the Strait of Gibraltar, where the Mediterranean Sea meets the Atlantic Ocean, and where Europe nearly touches the African continent at Morocco—Tunisia is the next closest point to Europe, lying about 100 miles (160 km) southwest of the Italian island of Sicily. This location made Tunisia an important stopping point for traders in the early seafaring days. The Gulfs of Tunis, Hammamet, and Gabes provided excellent natural harbors for warships and trading vessels, which made Tunisia very attractive to early conquerors. Through conquest and territorial proximity, Tunisia has been influenced by African, European, and Arab cultures, and today's Tunisians are a blend of these peoples.

For a relatively small country, Tunisia has a long coastline, giving it the highest ratio of coastline to surface area of any country in Africa. It also has great geographical diversity, made up of three major regions—the mountainous north, the central plains, and the desert south.

HOW AFRICA GOT ITS NAME

No one's really certain where the name Africa came from, but it seems that it did not come from any African people themselves. The ancient Romans first used the name Africa terra to describe the land that corresponds to modern-day Tunisia. This region, with its capital at the ancient city of Carthage (in today's Tunisia), was a province of the Roman Empire.

The name means "land of the Afri," after the Berber tribe, the Afri people (Afer in the singular formation). The name "Afer," in turn, may come from a Phoenician word for "dust," the name meaning "people of the dust." The name "Africa" might also be related to the Greek word aphrike, "without cold," and/or the Latin aprica, meaning "sunny." In medieval times, Tunisia was called Ifriqiya—the Arabic word for "Africa."

As Europeans further explored the enormous continent to their south, they expanded the name "Africa" to include more and more of the land. Tunisia, meanwhile, eventually came to be named after the city of Tunis that is now its capital.

TOPOGRAPHY

MOUNTAINOUS NORTH Occupying a quarter of the total land area, the mountainous north consists of two chains that are extensions of the Atlas Mountains of Algeria: the Northern Tell, or simply Tell, made up of the Kroumirie and Mogod mountains, and the High Tell or *Dorsale* (meaning "backbone"). The Northern Tell is more rugged than the Dorsale, but because both are made chiefly of soft sandstone and limestone, they have a lower, rounded profile compared with the sharp outlines of the Atlas Mountains west of Tunisia.

The few peaks that reach 5,000 feet (1,524 meters) are found in the Dorsale, near the Algerian border. The highest recorded peak in Tunisia is Djebel Chaambi (5,066 ft/1,544 m). The Medjerda, Teboursouk, and Tebéssa mountains in the Dorsale divide Tunisia into two distinct climatic regions: the well-watered Mediterranean north and the semiarid desert south.

Tunisia's mountainous valley region is verdant and lush.

Tunisia's longest and only river with a year-round flow of water is the Medjerda, which flows between the Northern Tell and the Dorsale. Rising from the Medjerda Mountains of northeast Algeria, it flows 290 miles (467 km) eastward to the Gulf of Tunis. The Medjerda River is used extensively for irrigation and to generate hydroelectric power, and its tributaries form the principal river system in Tunisia. The Medjerda Valley is richly covered with alluvium, making it extremely fertile. It has been the richest grain-producing region in the country since the period of ancient Roman rule.

Blessed with the richest soil of the country and a gentle climate, the mountainous north produces most of Tunisia's agricultural crops and is home to 50 percent of the nation's population.

CENTRAL PLAINS South of the mountains are plateaus ranging from 600 to 1,500 feet (180—450 m) high; elevations decrease toward the east. This semiarid region is named according to elevation, from west to east: high plains, low plains, and the *Sahel* (sa-HELL) along the eastern coast. The high plains are broad alluvial basins between low mountains, and the low plains are flat, gravel-covered plateaus. The Sahel includes a 200-mile (320-km) coastal strip and the islands of Djerba and Kerkenna. It has two distinct climatic areas: the northern, well-watered coast along the Gulf of Hammamet, and the southern, drier region along the Gulf of Gabes.

SOUTHERN DESERT Tunisia's desert begins just south of the plains and merges into the Sahara. The desert is bordered by an extensive depression containing three seasonal *chotts* or salt lakes: Chott el Djérid, Chott el Gharsa, and Chott el Fedjadj. In the high ground around the *chotts*, date palms grow abundantly in oases.

Tunisia's desert spreads over nearly half of its total land area, yet it forms only a tiny fraction of the Sahara, a bleak, desolate wasteland that covers a quarter of the continent of Africa. The desert terrain is characterized by drifting sand dunes from Algeria's Grand Erg Oriental, rocky areas, and mountain ridges of the flat-topped Ksour Mountains in the east. With the exception of scattered oases supplied by underground water, the southern desert is barren land.

The sand dunes of the Sahara Desert in Douz, Tunisia.

CLIMATE

Tunisia's climate is determined by the Mediterranean Sea, which brings cool breezes and moisture to the north, and by the Sahara, which sends hot, dusty winds blowing across the south. The climate varies in accordance with the three distinct terrains of mountains, plains, and desert.

The mountainous north has mild, wet winters (October—April) and hot, dry summers (May—September). Pleasant most of the time, winters can be uncomfortably cold, since central heating has been introduced only recently and is available only in newer buildings. Temperatures average 45° Fahrenheit (7° Celcius) in January and 80°F (27°C) in July. Rainfall averages 16 to 39 inches (40—100 cm) annually and occurs mainly in winter.

The semiarid central plains have little and unpredictable rainfall. Here summers are hot and winters are mild. Rainfall averages 8 to 16 inches (20—40 cm) annually and occurs mainly in winter. Temperatures on the coast of Sahel are moderated by the sea breezes, but the northern coast is cooler and wetter than the south, which is influenced by desert heat a few miles inland.

The temperature range is much greater in the desert, where summers are hotter and winters colder than elsewhere in Tunisia. Burning hot days (often over 100°F/38°C) are followed by cool evenings and cold nights. Rainfall is low, at 4 to 8 inches (10—20 cm) annually. Hot southerly winds called *sirocco* bring dreaded, blinding blizzards of sand blowing in from the Sahara.

FLORA AND FAUNA

Tunisia is an environmentally diverse country. Recently, government figures have listed 2,200 species of plants, 80 species of mammals, 67 species of reptiles and amphibians, and 362 species of birds as being native to the country. Scorpions are very common, with the most deadly species being the yellow fat-tailed scorpion, which often hides under stones or in the crevices of walls.

THE NORTH The cool, wet north, blessed with rich soil that is irrigated year-round by the Medjerda River, is the agricultural hub of the country.

Crops grown here include wheat, olives, grapes, citrus fruit, jasmine (for perfume), pistachios, jujube, and gum. The mountains are covered with wild juniper, myrtle, and laurel. The Kroumirie Mountains of northwest Tunisia are famous for their forests of cork oak.

The forested Northern Tell is the hunting ground of wild boars and jackals. In the Dorsale the sleeved mouflon (a species of wild sheep) and gazelles are seen. Migratory birds that fly south from Europe in the fall include aquatic and wading birds such as ducks, egrets, flamingos, geese, herons, and storks. Rapid urban expansion in northern Tunisia may result in a reduced number of migratory birds, particularly those that favor secluded habitats.

The rocky cliffs of Tunisia's northern mountains rise in the background while the lower slopes are dotted with olive groves.

THE CENTRAL AND COASTAL REGIONS In the arid plains, where the soil is poor, wild esparto grass is grown for manufacturing paper and rope. Grains, date palms, and olive trees are also cultivated in oases. There is little vegetation for animals other than nomadic herds of sheep, goats, and camels. Nomads use two kinds of camel: a stockier species to carry loads and long-legged ones that move fast.

The warm waters of Tunisia's coast, especially in the Gulf of Gabes, have more than 80 species of fish—including gilthead, sole, tuna, bonito, and shark—and sponges, octopuses, and shellfish. The northern coast is a coral haven for shrimp and lobsters. Monk seals are a protected species in the northern island sanctuary of Galite off the coastal town of Tabarka.

THE DESERT At oases, date palms grow in abundance, but elsewhere in the desert there is very little plant life. Plants that have adapted to the Tunisian

TUNISIA'S WORLD HERITAGE SITES

Tunisia has eight sites that have been designated as World Heritage Sites—seven cultural sites and one natural site. The United Nations Educational, Scientific and Cultural Organization (UNESCO) "seeks to encourage the identification, protection, and preservation of cultural and natural heritage around the world considered to be of outstanding value to humanity." To that end, the organization has compiled a list of cultural and natural World Heritage Sites, and considers additional sites for designation. In UNESCO's view, World Heritage Sites belong to all the peoples of the world, irrespective of the territory on which they are located."

Tunisia's places of outstanding value to humanity include:

- *Amphitheatre of El Jem, the ruins of the largest coliseum in North Africa dating to the third century.*

- *Archaeological Site of Carthage, with ancient ruins dating to the ninth century BCE.*

- *Medina of Tunis.*

- *Punic Town of Kerkuane and its Necropolis, ancient ruins located at the tip of Cape Bon, on a cliff overlooking the sea.*

- *Kairouan, an ancient Muslim holy city.*

- *Medina of Sousse, Tunisia's third largest city.*

- *Dougga / Thugga, ancient Roman ruins in northwestern Tunisia.*

- *Ichkeul National Park, which includes Lake Ichkeul, an important freshwater lake and wetlands area that supports hundreds of thousands of migratory birds.*

desert include the acacia with its long roots, scrub grass, saltbush, and cacti that store water in their fleshy stems. Ants, scarabs (a beetle species), scorpions, horned vipers, cobras, and lizards such as the skink and dab are common in the Sahara. Small animals include the fennec and the jerboa, also called the kangaroo rat because of its strong hind legs. Buzzards can be found in the desert, and migratory birds stop at oases.

MAJOR CITIES AND HISTORICAL SITES

Many of Tunisia's cities were founded centuries ago, and many include a medina quarter. The *medina* of a North African city is the old, Arab (non-European) district—a walled area filled with a labyrinth of passageways lined with shops, houses, and mosques. Tunisia's major cities, besides the capital Tunis, include Sfax, Sousse, Bizerte, and Kairouan.

TUNIS The economic and cultural capital of Tunisia, Tunis is also the most important port. It is built on Tunis Lake, which is connected to the Mediterranean by a human-made channel. Tunis was a small settlement during the Phoenician period and the early years of Arab rule (ninth century BCE to seventh century CE). It became a capital city under the Hafsids, a thirteenth-century Arab dynasty. In 1535 Spain, which was then at war with the Ottoman Empire, took possession of Tunis. The Turks repossessed it from 1539 until 1881, except for two years from 1573 to 1574, when Tunis was again occupied by Spain. Tunis became the capital of independent Tunisia in 1956.

A gateway called Bab el Bhar, or "Sea Gate," leads into the medina quarter of Tunis. New Tunis lies beyond this gate, built mostly on land that was reclaimed from the sea by the French during their rule, from 1881 to 1956.

Tunis is continually developing, and the pattern of settlement is uneven. One-third of the population lives in the old and cramped medina, while the

The white buildings of the Tunis medina seem to glow in this aerial view of the city. To the left is the high minaret of the Great Mosque.

remaining two-thirds are evenly distributed between makeshift homes on the outskirts of Tunis, built for nomads and those in search of jobs in the city, and the new city built by the French. The rich live comfortably in Belvedere, a former royal park situated a few miles from the city. Belvedere is well provided for by superb garden landscaping, waterfront cafés, a zoo, the Museum of Modern Art, a swimming pool, and a stadium.

SFAX This coastal city opposite the Kerkenna Islands is the second-largest city in Tunisia, and is a metropolis of the south. It is an economic center with a prominent commercial port. It is also important as an industrial, agricultural, and fishing town.

Talented architects have built futuristic buildings in the new sections of the town to rival the work of their competitors in Tunis. There are many jokes that tell of this competition, although with the migration of southerners to the northern capital city, the competitiveness has become less intense. Sfax became prosperous during Roman rule through growing, pressing, and shipping olive oil to its Mediterranean neighbors. This wealthy city caters to tourists with first-class hotels, shops, cafés, restaurants, and grand buildings. The eleventh-century Great Mosque has one of the finest minarets in Tunisia.

The beautiful buildings of Sfax include the city's town hall, at the right.

SOUSSE Tunisia's third-largest city, Sousse, is located 80 miles (130 km) north of Sfax and on the Gulf of Hammamet. It was formerly called Hadrumetum, and was a Phoenician town founded in the ninth century BCE. The name *Sousse* is derived from the word *Susah*, the ancient name for the town. Sousse, a thriving port and very popular seaside resort known for its white beaches, is often referred to as the "pearl of the coast." Many kinds of leisure activities are offered here, including diving, horseback riding, sailing, and golfing.

Like many other Tunisian cities, Sousse has an intriguing blend of old and new districts. The medina of Sousse is a World Heritage Site. The National Museum, which is second in importance only to the Bardo Museum in Tunis, has collections that record scenes from the Roman and Byzantine periods (from the first to the sixth centuries CE).

BIZERTE Its strategic location at the northernmost point in North Africa, after the Strait of Gibraltar, decided Bizerte's destiny as a military outpost. Bizerte was known as Hippo Diarrhytus in Phoenician and Roman times, and the Arabs gave its modern name when they conquered it in the seventh century CE. When Tunisia became a French protectorate, a channel was built linking Lake Bizerte to the Mediterranean Sea, making Bizerte a naval base. Bizerte's military role ended in 1963 when the French naval base was evacuated and the city was returned to independent Tunisia.

KAIROUAN About 80 miles (130 km) south of Tunis lies Kairouan, the fourth most important Islamic city in the world, after Mecca, Medina, and Jerusalem. Seven visits to Kairouan are considered equivalent to one pilgrimage to Mecca, the birthplace of the Prophet Muhammad.

Uqba ibn Nafi, whose armies entered North Africa from the south on a quest to conquer territory and spread Islam to the Maghreb, founded Kairouan in 670 CE. Kairouan, surrounded by salt lakes and dry land, was an inhospitable place. Muslims believe that when the city was founded, a miraculous stream appeared at the bottom of a well, filling it with water from the Zem Zem spring in Mecca, thousands of miles away.

A legend surrounds the founding of the ancient Phoenician city of Carthage by Elissa-Dido, the shrewd queen of Tyre (in modern Lebanon). She fled from her brother, King Pygmalion, in the ninth century BCE, after he murdered her husband. Arriving in the region of Carthage, she tricked the inhabitants into giving her land. They agreed that she could have an amount of land that did not exceed the size of a cow's hide. She outwitted them by cutting the hide into thousands of fine strips, which she tied end-to-end to form an extremely long rope to encircle the Hill of Byrsa.

Carthage, or Kart-Hadasht *(Phoenician for "New City"), was founded in 814 BCE.*

Carthage became the first naval power in the Mediterranean to conquer parts of Spain and Italy and expand into Africa. This strategic control of the Mediterranean threatened Roman supremacy and resulted in three wars with Rome (the Punic Wars—264–241, 218–201, and 149–146 BCE). After the final battle, the victorious Romans razed the city and covered the site with salt so that no crops could grow. The survivors were enslaved and deported.

Qairwan, the Arabic name for Kairouan, may be the source of the word "caravan." The city is strategically located on the old caravan trail that linked Egypt with the Maghreb.

Kairouan is famous for its beautiful, imposing mosques and the centuries-old art of carpet weaving. The city's main attraction is the Great Mosque, the first mosque built in North Africa by the conqueror Uqba ibn Nafi in the seventh century CE to house Arabic, Greek, and Islamic literature. Seven doors in the fortress-like walls open into the courtyard to reveal the mosque's amazing beauty. From the white marbled courtyard, visitors enter a prayer room through one of seventeen carved cedar doors that lead to a forest of 414 multi-colored marble and porphyry columns. Kairouan is listed as a UNESCO World Heritage Site.

BULLA REGIA   This is an ancient town built in tiers on the slopes of a mountain some 25 miles (40 km) southwest of Béja, a town along the Medjerda River. Many ruins remain here, including Roman baths, the temples of Apollo and Isis, a theater, a Byzantine Christian basilica and baptistery, and unusual underground houses with names such as Palaces of Hunting and Fishing and the House of the Peacock.

CAPE BON PENINSULA This peninsula in the northeast has exotic gardens, thermal springs believed to have curative powers, beaches, and popular shopping areas. Hammamet and Nabeul are two towns on the peninsula.

Nabeul is famous for its arts and crafts, ceramics, orange flower water, and embroidered cloth. The Museum of Nabeul has rare statues and ancient earthenware and a fine collection of antique lamps, ceramics, and mosaics. Nabeul is at its prettiest in spring when the city celebrates a festival of orange blossoms around the end of March and early April.

Hammamet, a small seaside resort town lined with citrus trees, lies south of Nabeul. Its sandy white beaches and warm weather attract vacationing Europeans and Tunisians. The medina is especially lovely, painted in pastel colors.

INTERNET LINKS

https://www.britannica.com/place/Tunisia
This site presents a good overview of Tunisia's geography.

**https://www.cia.gov/library/publications/the-world-factbook/
geos/ts.html**
Facts about Tunisia's geography are listed on this site.

http://whc.unesco.org/en/list/&order=country#alphaT
The links to the World Heritage Sites for Tunisia are on this UNESCO page.

HISTORY

A national monument to independence rises in the public
square in front of the New Town Hall in Tunis.

2

HUMAN HISTORY GOES WAY BACK IN North Africa, which makes sense since Africa is where the human species first emerged. Archaeologists have excavated two-million-year-old stone tools in the Maghreb. In the early Stone Age, the inhabitants of Tunisia were hunters, fishers, growers, and gatherers. Little else is known of their existence before the Phoenicians—people from the easternmost lands of the Mediterranean Sea—arrived in the twelfth century BCE. Historical events in Tunisia since then have been influenced by the country's strategic position along the Mediterranean route between Europe and Asia.

Phoenician traders established settlements on Tunisia's northeast coast. One of them, Carthage, founded in the ninth century BCE, grew to encompass most of present-day Tunisia by the sixth century BCE. Carthage's growing power challenged Rome, another contender for Mediterranean supremacy, and the city changed hands in the second

In 2014, in the wake of the 2011 revolution, Tunisian President Moncef Marzouki launched the Truth and Dignity Commission, headed by human rights activist Slhem Bensedrine. Its purpose is to investigate human rights violations committed by the government since 1955. By June 2016, the commission gathered 62,000 submissions and heard testimony from some 11,000 people.

century BCE. It stayed under Roman rule until the fifth century CE, when the Vandals and, later, the Byzantines came to power.

In the seventh century CE, the Arabs brought Islam to Tunisia; this marked the beginning of five Arab dynasties in Tunisia. Regardless of who has had control of the area since then, Tunisia has remained an important part of the Islamic world. In the beginning of the sixteenth century, the Spanish commanded some coastal areas, speeding up the decline of the last Arab dynasty. The Ottoman Turks conquered the territory in 1574 and held it until their own decline in the late nineteenth century.

A political tussle in Europe for strategic control over Tunisia ended with France making Tunisia a French protectorate in 1881. Tunisia finally became a self-governing country on July 25, 1957.

PHOENICIAN RULE

In the twelfth century BCE, Phoenicians from Tyre (now Lebanon) established settlements on the North African coast to service their ships sailing between Tyre and Spain, a source of tin and silver. According to legend, in 814 BCE, Elissa-Dido founded a settlement in North Africa called Kart-Hadasht, or Carthage. Unlike the other Phoenician settlements, Carthage was politically independent. It grew powerful partly in response to Greek attempts to drive the Phoenicians out of Sicily. By the third century BCE, Carthage controlled Sicily, Sardinia, Corsica, Spain, and Africa. Fearful of this rival power in the Mediterranean, Rome began a campaign of war against Carthage. The Punic Wars, as they came to be called, spanned 118 years.

FIRST PUNIC WAR (264—241 BCE) Rome's opportunity came in 264 BCE when Messina and Syracuse, two Sicilian cities, quarreled over control of Messina. Carthage settled the dispute and occupied Messina, but a Roman army forced the Carthaginians to withdraw. Rome took over Corsica in 260 BCE, and, four years later, established its army at Clypea in Africa (modern-day Kelibia in Tunisia). Plagued by internal revolts, Carthage nonetheless repelled the Romans in 256 BCE. Eventually, in 241 BCE, with a superior fleet of two hundred warships, Rome emerged victorious.

Over the next two decades, Rome captured Carthaginian territory in Corsica and Sardinia without retaliation, but Carthage began to extend its empire into Spain, where General Hamilcar Barca founded the settlements of Alicante and Barcino (modern Barcelona). Two Carthaginian leaders succeeded Hamilcar—his son Hannibal and son-in-law Hasdrubal. In 219 BCE, Hannibal captured Saguntum (modern-day Sagunto) in Spain, and Rome once again declared war.

This nineteenth century engraving of the Battle of Zama (202 BCE), in the Second Punic War shows Hannibal's war elephants.

SECOND PUNIC WAR (218—201 BCE) The Romans controlled the sea, so Hannibal's army, which famously included war elephants, crossed overland and through the Alps to Italy in 218 BCE. His army inflicted costly losses on the Roman Empire, capturing the city of Capua in southern Italy. The Romans blocked reinforcements led by Hasdrubal and recaptured Capua in 211 BCE. In 203 BCE, Hannibal returned to Africa. Meanwhile the Romans attacked Carthaginian strongholds in Spain and northern Africa. Carthage was defeated in Spain by 206 BCE, and Hannibal's army was defeated at Zama in central Tunisia in 202 BCE. Carthage was forced to pay huge reparations to Rome.

THIRD PUNIC WAR (149—146 BCE) The Carthaginians recovered their prosperity and paid off their war debt in ten years. A vengeful Rome found an excuse for a new war when Carthage broke the peace agreement in 150 BCE by going to war with Rome's ally, the Numidian prince Massinissa. After three years, a besieged Carthage fell in just eight days of fierce fighting. Rome ruled the entire region previously held by Carthage.

ROMAN RULE AND BEYOND

The Roman province included modern Tunisia and parts of Libya and Algeria. Rome promoted agriculture here, and Roman engineers designed aqueducts to bring water from the mountains to the coast to irrigate the land for crops such as wheat, grapes, and olives. Tunisia became the granary, or "breadbasket" of Rome because it grew millions of tons of grains each year, which were then exported to Rome and its territories.

Rome adopted Christianity as the official religion in 380 CE under the emperor Theodosius (reigned 379—395 CE). In the years that followed,

Ruins of Roman aqueduct arches near Carthage are evidence of Tunisia's ancient history.

however, the Roman Empire began to decline. Plagued by internal troubles, the Romans could not defend its North Africa province from the Vandals. Germanic warriors—Aryan Christians who wore horsehair jackets and lived in tents—conquered Carthage in 439 and established a Vandal kingdom in North Africa that lasted for the another century. Ultimately, however, the Vandal occupation failed, and the region fell under the rule of the Byzantine Empire. Like the Vandals, the Byzantines tried to alter the type of Christianity being practiced in the African province. Christianity was still in its formative years, and disputes between different Catholic sects caused religious discord throughout the Byzantine Empire. For the most part, the Berber people in Tunisia remained loyal to their own tribal confederacies.

THE ARABS BRING ISLAM

Great change came to North Africa with the Arab invasions of the seventh and eleventh centuries. With them, the Arabs brought the world's newest religion, Islam, founded by the Prophet Muhammad in what is today Saudi Arabia. By the time of his death in 632, Prophet Muhammad and his followers had spread Islam to most of the Arabian Peninsula. In 670, the Arabs moved westward and founded the city of Kairouan some 100 miles (160 km) south of Carthage, in the old Roman province the Arabs called *Ifriqiya*.

Unlike the Romans, Vandals, and Byzantines, the Arabs came as conquerors and missionaries, not as colonists. They intermarried with the Berbers, spreading Arab culture, the Arabic language, and the religion of Islam to the indigenous people. The Berbers, for their part, simply adapted Islam to their local culture, but maintained their own identity somewhat separate from the eastern Arabs.

Various Arabic dynasties—the Umayyads, the Abbasids, the Aghlabids, and the Fatimids—controlled Tunisia as part of their extended empire from 661 to 1044. Under these ruling dynasties, Muslim culture spread west across Northern Africa to Morocco and north into Spain.

By the seventh century, two Islamic groups had evolved, and they exist today—the Sunni and Shia. The Shia Muslims believe that only direct descendants of the Prophet Muhammad should rule. The Sunni Muslims believe that Islamic rulers should be elected from among those capable of the job. The Abbasids were Sunnis, as were the Aghlabids. The religious leaders they elected were often proud nobles who did not identify with the poor non-Arabs. This created resentment, and when taxes became a burden, opposition grew among the Berbers, who supported the Fatimids, a Shia group that claimed to be the descendants of Fatima, the Prophet Muhammad's daughter.

MUSLIM BERBER DOMINATION

Fatimid rule (910—1044) was harsh and intolerant, but trade developed quickly. European demand for Eastern goods made Fatimid-controlled areas in Ifriqiya and Sicily important distribution centers. Trading houses opened all over Ifriqiya, dealing in spices, lacquer, dyes, grain, drugs, and cloth woven from Egyptian flax.

Other Berber Muslim dynasties controlled the Maghreb region in the centuries to follow, the Almoravids (1062—1147) and the Almohads (1130—1269). Shifts of power often sparked years of conflict, political instability, and economic decline, which accounts for some of the overlap in power over such a large territory.

The Almohads ruled North Africa and Spain from 1130 to 1269. The Almohad court was a center of art and Arabic learning, yet the empire soon crumbled because of its great size, social divisions, and religious conservatism. Ongoing wars in Spain, where Christians were trying to retake the region, drained its resources.

The Hafsids ruled the region for more than three hundred years, from 1207 to 1574. One of the rulers of that dynasty, the poet-prince Abu Zakariya al Hafs (reigned 1228—1249), moved the capital from Kairouan to Tunis, and renamed Ifriqiya "Tunisia."

The Hafsids concentrated on the coastal towns, coexisting with the Berbers by leaving the inland areas to them. Stability returned to the area. Trade links were developed and ambassadors were exchanged with European states. There was a cultural revival, and the Zituna Mosque in Tunis, with

THE CRUSADES

In 1095, the Catholic Pope Urban II called for Christians throughout Europe to wrest the Holy Land—Jerusalem and the surrounding region—from Muslim control. A series of military offensives, or holy wars, followed over the next two hundred years, with generally dismal results. Many of these wars were particularly brutal. The Crusades, as they came to be called, sparked religious fervor among European Christians that eventually broadened beyond their original goal of recovering the Holy Lands. Later crusades undertook to fight enemies of the faith wherever they were found, and this came to mean Muslims in general—and stopping the expansion of Islam into Europe.

"The Siege of Tunis," an eighteenth-century engraving by John Harris.

In 1270, King Louis IX of France launched a crusade against the city of Tunis, with the ultimate goal of conquering Egypt. The Siege of Tunis was a disaster—an epidemic of dysentery swept through the ranks as Louis' men waited in Carthage for additional contingents to arrive. Louis' son John Tristan died there of the illness, and Louis himself did as well a few weeks later. Despite his crusade's failure, Louis was eventually canonized, or recognized as a saint, by the Catholic Church.

In general, the Crusades did not accomplish their goal, though they did help to prevent the spread of Islam into Europe. However, the wars deeply embittered Muslim Christian relations, in ways that are still felt today. Some Muslims tend to equate Western imperialism—such as France's nineteenth- and twentieth-century domination of Tunisia—and other foreign initiatives with a continuation of the Crusades.

BARBARY PIRATES

A Turkish-Greek corsair, or pirate, nicknamed Barbarossa, or "Redbeard" in Italian, became a legendary figure in the Mediterranean around this time. He and his brothers

reached Tunisia in 1504. In 1510 the ruler of Algiers asked the brothers to defend it from the Spanish. Instead they conquered Algiers and made it and the other coastal countries a base for their piracy against European shipping in the Mediterranean. These countries, including Tunisia, came to be called the Barbary States.

The Turks went into an informal partnership with pirates to gain naval supremacy in the Mediterranean Sea. Piracy brought handsome profits from raids on ships and coastal towns and from the ransoming or sale of hostages. Trading powers also began to bribe the pirates to ensure safe travel. This situation lasted for several centuries.

Following the independence of the United States, the British Navy no longer protected American ships, and many American crewmen were captured and enslaved by pirates off the North African coast. In 1800, the United States signed a treaty with the Ottoman ruler, promising that the United States would pay an annual tribute (cash) in return for immunity from attack by Tunisian-based pirates. In 1805, a Tunisian mission to Washington DC, exchanged the tribute for a trade agreement. A joint agreement signed by Britain, France, and Tunisia in 1818 made it illegal to arm pirates or to take Christians as slaves. However, the piracy didn't end until the French conquest of Algeria in 1830.

its library of thirty-six thousand Islamic texts, became the center of Islamic learning in the Maghreb.

In the fifteenth century, the war between Spain and the Ottoman Turks came to Tunis. The Hafsids supported the Spanish in a war that lasted fifty years.

RULE OF THE OTTOMAN TURKS

Tunisia was assimilated into the Turkish Ottoman Empire in the sixteenth century and became a center of Arab culture and learning. The Ottomans divided the Maghreb into administrative units called regencies.

A governor called a pasha, who was allowed no political power, headed the regency of Tunis. The Janissaries, members of an elite corps of the Ottoman army kept order and reported to officers called *dey*. The dey collected taxes in the coastal towns, while a civilian *bey* controlled Berber tribes inland with a private army.

The bey of Tunis was the effective ruler of Tunisia, although Tunisia remained part of the Ottoman Empire. Under the beys, trade and foreign relations developed, but economic and security problems increased spending. Tunisia's wealth was also used for the beys' private spending, and taxes from one-third of the population were not collected because the army was afraid to travel to the remote regions where the Berbers lived.

Ahmad Ibn Mustafa (1806—1855), also called Ahmad Bey, started a modernization program based on the Western model. He introduced military reform so that Tunisians could be trained to defend their own country and he bought military hardware. A supporter of social reforms, he abolished slavery and outlawed discrimination against Jews.

Tunisia paid dearly for Ahmad Bey's ambitious plans and for the embezzlement of funds by his prime minister, Mustapha Khaznadar. The bankrupt government borrowed heavily from Britain, France, and Italy. These countries, particularly France, used Tunisia's debt to gain political influence. To reorganize Tunisia's finances, an International Financial Commission (IFC) was set up in Tunis in 1869, represented by Tunisia, Britain, France, and Italy. Tunisia was stripped of its independence: Foreign relations were given up to the Ottoman Empire, and economic affairs to the IFC. Only internal matters remained under the control of the bey. France began its economic domination of Tunisia by establishing French-owned companies to buy land for development. By the time the French protectorate was established, French economic control was complete.

THE FRENCH PROTECTORATE

At the Berlin Congress of 1874, the European powers divided Africa among themselves. Britain recognized France's control over Tunisia in return for control over Cyprus. All France needed was an excuse to occupy Tunisia. That excuse came in 1881, when, claiming to be pursuing Tunisian Kroumirie tribesmen who had crossed the border to raid Algeria, France invaded Tunisia. A force of thirty-six thousand French troops headed for the bey's palace in Tunis, while the French Navy seized Bizerte—both far from the scene of the alleged raid.

Power over Tunisia's foreign relations and finances was surrendered to France. The French appointed a minister to serve as an advisor to the bey. Tunisian uprisings to protest French intervention resulted in France's capture of the cities of Sousse, Gafsa, Gabes, and Kairouan. French control over Tunisia was made complete with the signing of the 1883 Convention of La Marsa, a treaty that allowed the dynasty of the beys to continue, with the French ruling through them.

COLONIZATION The 1883 treaty gave the French powers to introduce administrative, judicial, and financial reforms to Tunisia. A modernization program followed, along with efficient tax collection. Roads, railways, hospitals, schools, and modern sanitation works were built, and ports were improved. The French took the best agricultural land. With their technology and financial expertise, the French were able to reintroduce the large-scale cultivation of olives and grapes that had existed centuries before. These crops and Tunisia's mineral reserves were tapped for export.

The justice system was reformed, with the *shariah* (Islamic) courts handling only personal matters of marriage and inheritance, while other

Kherredin Pasha, a Mamluk from Circassia (modern-day Russia), drew up Tunisia's constitution in 1861. It provided for a limited hereditary monarchy, with the bey as head of state and the prime minister as head of government. The new government was answerable to a supreme council, which was responsible for financial, administrative, legal, and military matters. The constitution gave a secular court the power to review shariah court judgments. The urban elite supported the constitution, but the majority rejected it. A serious tribal rebellion caused the constitution to be suspended in 1864, but Tunisians harked back to this constitution of 1861 in their march toward nationalism a century later.

In 1873 Kherredin Pasha became prime minister. He planned economic reforms that would have helped Tunisians, but they threatened European interests. In 1877, through France's instigation, Kherredin was dismissed, to be replaced by a leader who would be more easily controlled by the French.

matters were addressed by the French legal code. Two appeal courts were set up, the first in Algiers and the second in Paris, France. French became the official language, and military service was made compulsory for Tunisians and French people living in Tunisia.

Changing the rural society to a commercial and urban one brought about a social revolution in Tunisia. Land reform created difficulties for both the French and Tunisians. Traditionally land was owned collectively and represented wealth to the Tunisians. First Islamic rules governing land inheritance brought complications, and then the French changed communal ownership to individual ownership. Wealth shifted to those who were able to work the land most productively. Tunisians had difficulty adjusting to this change, since their resources of money, education, and tools were much poorer than those of their European counterparts. Modernization, it seemed, benefited the elite and not the masses.

THE RISE OF NATIONALISM

In 1890 a small Western-educated group called the Young Tunisians began to demand more reforms and greater Tunisian participation in government.

In 1907 they promoted their ideas through their own French language newspaper, *Le Tunisien*. Sheikh Taalbi, one of the leaders of the group, wrote a widely distributed book demanding that reforms be made. This spurred the formation, after World War I, of the Destour (Constitutional) Party. Its members belonged to the conservative elite: men who were well educated and wealthy. In 1920 the Destour Party called for the reinstatement of the constitution of 1861, with some changes. It was essentially a demand for a constitutional form of government where Tunisians and Europeans would have equal rights.

The French responded with repression, arresting the leader of the Destour Party. The bey threatened to abdicate if the Destour reforms were not accepted, and French troops promptly surrounded his palace. Only minor reforms were conceded. Disillusioned by the failure of the Destour Party, younger, middle-class nationalists started a new party, the Neo-Destour (New Constitutional), in 1934. They found a more aggressive leader in Habib ali Bourguiba, a French-educated Tunisian lawyer. French attempts to suppress the Neo-Destour Party only increased its popularity. Its leader, Bourguiba, was exiled and imprisoned several times during the course of the fight for independence.

WORLD WAR II AND INDEPENDENCE

Germany occupied France during World War II, and the Germans fought in Tunisia for six months starting in November 1942. When the Axis Powers (Germany and its allies) were defeated in North Africa in 1943, Tunisia again came under the control of the French. The Tunisians expected to gain their independence as a natural consequence of supporting the French during the war, but they were wrong. The French deposed the bey and tried to capture Bourguiba, who fled to Egypt in 1945, where he continued his campaign for Tunisian independence.

Realizing that the political climate was changing in Europe's colonial possessions, however, in 1951 the French finally allowed the formation of a government in Tunisia that included some nationalist leaders. When the Tunisians urged a faster pace toward the formation of a parliament, French repression returned. Nationalist groups went underground and popular demonstrations increased, accompanied by sporadic acts of terrorism.

In July 1954, the French promised to guide Tunisia toward independence. Bourguiba, who had been permitted to return to the country in September 1949, only to be confined at the outbreak of rebellion, supervised the convention, which was signed in 1955. The result was limited self-rule. Most Neo-Destour members rejected the offer, but Bourguiba accepted the agreement as a stepping-stone to independence. On March 20, 1956, Tunisia was pronounced independent with a constitutional monarchy ruled by the bey. At the first national legislative elections, the Neo-Destour Party won the majority of seats and Habib Bourguiba became president of the National Assembly.

In 1957 the assembly adopted a constitution that ended the rule of the beys. Tunisia adopted a constitution modeled on the French system, which established the basic outline of the highly centralized presidential system that continues today. The military was given a defined defensive role, which excluded participation in politics.

THE BOURGUIBA ERA

President Bourguiba placed strong emphasis on education, the status of women, and the creation of jobs, and Tunisia enjoyed strong social progress. The literacy and school attendance rates rose, population growth slowed, and poverty rates fell. For the most part, the economy grew steadily, and the president was popular. He was reelected in 1964, 1969, and 1974.

In 1975, Bourguiba became "president for life," by way of a constitutional amendment. The Neo-Destour Party, renamed the Socialist Destourian Party, was the only legal political organization; all other parties were banned. To win the cooperation of traditional Islamic elements, Bourguiba declared Islam the state religion. However, he modified the Islamic institutions of education, justice, medical services, and the status of women in accordance with his more liberal and even secularist interpretation of Islam.

Habib Bourguiba hoists the flag of Tunisia on March 22, 1956, to mark the country's new independence.

The Code of Personal Status was passed, giving wives the legal power to institute divorce proceedings against their husbands. Polygamy was outlawed, even though Islamic law permits a Muslim man to have up to four wives, and abortion and birth control were legalized. The powers of the shariah courts were neutralized and turned over to the civil courts. Distinctions between religious and public schools were abolished. Women were encouraged to enter all trades and professions. In 1984 two women were included in Bourguiba's cabinet.

Many Muslim countries struggle with friction between those who hold fundamentalist, or conservative views, and those who follow a more liberal, modern interpretation of Islam. Fundamentalists believe Islamic law should govern all personal, social, and political aspects of life. Bourguiba's reforms challenged traditionalist ideals. Opposition from the Islamic fundamentalists grew, leading to riots and plots against the government.

An economic slump in 1982 to 1983 also led to riots and strikes during which one hundred people were killed and trade union leaders were arrested. The government took tighter control and put a stiffer rein on the opposition as Bourguiba grew increasingly conservative and paranoid. He reshuffled his cabinet, getting rid of loyal aides. For a while, he even turned against his wife and son.

In 1987, the government rounded up Islamic fundamentalists, who were tried by a state security court and found guilty of terrorist activities and plotting against the government. Bourguiba named the minister of the interior, General Zine El Abidine Ben Ali, who conducted this crackdown, prime minister in 1987.

THE BEN ALI REGIME

In November of that year, Ben Ali was sworn in as president after seven doctors declared that Bourguiba was senile and too ill to rule. Ben Ali ruled Tunisia as president, winning the elections in 1994, 1999, and October 2004. He brought political stability, but did it by clamping down on dissent. On the other hand, he delivered steady economic growth to Tunisia, forging closer links with the European Union and the United States.

At first Ben Ali followed a policy of national reconciliation, releasing political prisoners who had been locked up under the previous regime. He also introduced political reforms that allowed opposition parties to compete openly in elections for the first time since Tunisia gained its independence.

In 1989, Ben Ali won 99 percent of the presidential vote, and repeated this remarkable electoral success during elections in 1994 and 1999. However, such overwhelming victories raised red flags. In 2002 Ben Ali's government changed the constitution to allow a president to stay in power until the age of seventy-five and be re-elected an unlimited number of times—effectively making himself president for life.

Ben Ali's regime was widely criticized both inside and outside of Tunisia for harassing opposition leaders and limiting freedom of the press. Ben Ali's government also took a hard line against Islamic extremists. After a bomb attack on a synagogue in Djerba killed twenty-one people in 2002, dozens of suspected Islamist militants were killed in shoot-outs with the police and hundreds of suspects were arrested.

In October 2004, Ben Ali was again re-elected, this time with a reported 94.5 percent of the vote. The main opposition group, the Democratic Progressive Party, pulled out of the elections just a few days before the vote, saying that its participation would only help legitimize a flawed democratic process.

REVOLUTION

On December 17, 2010, a young produce vendor in the central Tunisian city of Sidi Bouzid found he simply couldn't take any more abuse. The unemployed university graduate had been trying to support a family of eight by peddling fruits and vegetables. Humiliated, harassed, and fined almost daily by the local authorities, Mohamed Bouazizi sat in front of the provincial headquarters, doused himself with gasoline, and lit a match.

Bouazizi did not die right away, but lingered in the hospital for more than two weeks, finally succumbing to his horrific injuries on January 4, 2011. Meanwhile, his story spread across the region by way of social media, and people reacted with rage. Many took to the streets to protest the widespread police brutality that had triggered Bouazizi's despair, but the grievances

> ## THE ARAB SPRING

When the uprising in Tunisia resulted in the exile of a despised dictator, people in other countries took note. Pro-democracy advocates rose up across the heavily authoritarian Arab world. Hoping for governmental reforms leading to increased freedom, demonstrators took to the streets—which is an unusual event in Arab countries. Social media such as Twitter played an important role in getting the message out, particularly in nations where the media was state controlled.

At first, there was a sense of history being made, not unlike the downfall of the Soviet Union in 1989. In some instances—in Egypt, for example—the uprisings did result in regime change. Egypt's President Hosni Mubarak was quickly overthrown after his thirty-year rule. In other places, such as Algeria, Jordan, and Oman, the government agreed to certain reforms to quell the uprisings. Western media dubbed the phenomenon the "Arab Spring," though the term was never embraced by the Arab world itself.

By mid-2012, however, the wave of popular dissent died down, dampened by violent responses from authorities. Some uprisings escalated into large-scale conflicts, such as the Syrian and Libyan civil wars. In many places where old regimes were toppled, the resulting power vacuums led to chaos, opening the door to new dictatorships.

Several years after the Arab Spring, many observers concluded that not much had been gained, and not much had changed. For one thing, the protesters had a number of different agendas and visions, which often conflicted. In more secular Muslim countries, ironically, the old, corrupt despots had largely kept the Islamist insurgencies under control. With them gone, the fundamentalist religious militants rose up—most significantly, the Islamic State (ISIS)—particularly in Syria, Iraq, Yemen, and Tunisia's neighbor, Libya.

Some analysts refer to this period of ongoing conflicts as the "Arab Winter." As of July 2017, the only country to have emerged from the Arab Spring with a transition to constitutional democratic governance is the one that started it all—Tunisia.

quickly expanded to include the Ben Ali regime, government corruption, poor economic conditions, and political oppression. Police responded by beating and killing hundreds of protesters, which only fueled the mass fury. To try to quell the uproar, President Ben Ali—who had been ignoring the protests—finally went to see Bouazizi in the hospital on December 28. But the visit only stoked public indignation.

Violence erupted. Lawyers and teachers went on strike. On January 10, all schools and universities were closed indefinitely. On January 14, just ten days after Bouazizi died, Ben Ali fled the country.

AFTERMATH

The revolution did not quiet down immediately. Chaos and violence was eventually brought under control and the country began its difficult transition from authoritarian rule to a more democratic form of government. In 2014, Tunisian representatives wrote and approved a new constitution; and later that year, the country held its first free presidential election.

Tunisia's tenuous grasp on order and normalcy has been tested by terror attacks, particularly two in 2015 that targeted tourists. The tourism sector of the country's economy was severely damaged as a result, further adding to economic woes which undermine peace.

INTERNET LINKS

http://www.aljazeera.com/indepth/features/2011/01/2011126121815985483.html
This article traces the events that led to the Tunisian Revolution.

http://www.bbc.com/news/world-africa-14107720
The BBC News presents a timeline of important events in the history of Tunisia.

https://www.britannica.com/place/Tunisia/History
Britannica provides an up-to-date overview of Tunisian history.

http://www.newyorker.com/magazine/2016/03/28/tunisia-and-the-fall-after-the-arab-spring
This article looks at the growing problem of jihadism among Tunisian youths.

GOVERNMENT

Tunisia's National Constituent Assembly meets in 2012 to draw up a new constitution.

3

TUNISIA IS A PARLIAMENTARY republic, a representative democracy in which power is shared by a president, who is the head of state, and a prime minister, who is the head of government. Since gaining independence from France in 1956, the government has been based on a constitution, of which there have been several versions. The current constitution was written in 2014, after the Tunisian revolution ousting longtime president Zine El Abidine Ben Ali in January 2011.

THE CONSTITUTION

The rewriting of the constitution after the demise of the Ben Ali regime was the country's first attempt to legally define what the new, post-revolution Tunisia should be. Naturally, there were many points of view on that topic, and the process of finding consensus took several years. During that time, two high-profile, progressive politicians were assassinated.

The new constitution, finally adopted in 2014, addresses the general principals upon which the country is founded, the rights and freedoms of its citizens, and the authority and structure of the government. It establishes Tunisia as "a republican, democratic and participatory system, in the framework of a civil state founded on the sovereignty of the people." It calls for respect for human rights, but does put some restrictions on free speech. In particular, it bans attacks on religion and prohibits making accusations of "Takfir"—that is, one Muslim calling another Muslim a non-believer. Such an accusation, especially when used against leaders of Islamic states, can be seen as a justification for violence, which the Tunisian constitution expressly prohibits.

The constitution also provides for gender equality in rights and responsibilities, calls for protecting the nation's natural resources, and demands the government take steps to fight corruption. In the Preamble, the document affirms Tunisia's commitment to Arab unity, particularly among the people of the Maghreb, opposes all forms of colonization and racism, and specifically calls for the liberation of Palestine.

GOVERNMENT LEADERS

Executive authority in Tunisia lies with the president and the prime minister. The president is the head of state and commander-in-chief of the army. He or she must be a Muslim, a Tunisian citizen from birth, and at least thirty-five years old. In an effort to fight corruption, the new constitution requires the president, prime minister, minsters, and members of the parliament to disclose their assets.

The Tunisian people elect the president every five years by means of "universal, free, direct, secret, fair, and transparent elections," according to the constitution. The voting age is eighteen. The president wins by an absolute majority. If on the first round, no candidate achieves an absolute majority, the two candidates with the highest number of votes run again in a second election within two weeks. The new constitution limits presidents to two consecutive terms, and reinforces that stipulation with a barrier to future amendments—"The constitution may not be amended to increase the number or the length of presidential terms."

TUNISIA'S CONSTITUTION: STATE AND RELIGION

Many Muslim countries struggle with political friction between those who hold fundamentalist, or conservative, views and those who follow a more liberal, modern interpretation of Islam. (The relationship between religion and government is a common concern in many non-Muslim countries as well.) Fundamentalists believe Islamic law should govern all personal, social, and political aspects of life. Progressives, while personally devoted to Islam, take a somewhat more cosmopolitan view.

Tunisia's new constitution, adopted in 2014, addresses the question of religion right away. The constitution asserts that Islam is the official state religion; that the state is the "guardian of religion," but yet establishes freedom of religion. Some observers might view this as a tricky balancing act for any government.

However, the constitution is not neutral on the issue of religion—the document itself is framed in reference to God. Its opening words are, "In the Name of God, the Merciful, the Compassionate..." and its final words state, "...God is the guarantor of success."

Article 1 states, "Tunisia is a free, independent, sovereign state; its religion is Islam, its language Arabic, and its system is republican." It goes on to say "This article may not be amended." This means any future change to these tenets would require throwing out the entire constitution.

Article 6 says, "The state is the guardian of religion. It guarantees freedom of conscience and belief, the free exercise of religious practices and the neutrality of mosques and places of worship from all partisan [intervention]." This article goes on to affirm the government's commitment to "moderation and tolerance," the "protection of the sacred," and its opposition to "the incitement of violence and hatred."

انتخابات **2014** | Élections présidentielles | الإنتخابات الرئاسية

44.32% | 55.68%

محمد منصف المرزوقي | الباجي قايد السبسي

Tunisia's elections officials announce the winner of the 2014 presidential election, Beji Caid Essebsi (right, on the large screen behind them).

In the 2014 presidential election, Beji Caid Essebsi, a former prime minister and head of the Nidaa Tounes ("Call of Tunisia") party, became Tunisia's first freely and directly elected president under the new constitution. However, Essebsi, born in 1926, was eighty-seven years old when he assumed his position; at this writing in 2017, he is one of the world's oldest heads of state. The next election is scheduled for 2019.

The prime minister, as head of government, is nominated by the majority party in parliament and is appointed by the president. In 2016, President Essebsi named Youssef Chahed (b. 1975) as prime minister after the previous prime minister, Habib Essid, lost a vote of confidence in the parliament. Like the president, Chahed is a member of the Nidaa Tounes Party. He is also an agricultural engineer, researcher, and university professor, and speaks fluent Arabic, French, English, and Italian.

SHARIAH LAW

Shariah, or Islamic law, is derived from many sources—the Qur'an, the teachings of the Prophet Muhammad, and the interpretations of Islamic legal experts. In shariah courts, Muslim judges rule according to shariah law. Prior to the French protectorate, shariah law was applied to all Tunisians and in all situations.

During the French protectorate, shariah courts existed with limited powers. They ruled only in cases of marriage, divorce, inheritance, and land ownership. A secular court system to cover criminal and commercial matters was created for all Tunisians.

After independence shariah courts were abolished and the 1957 Code of Personal Status was adopted for all Muslims.

THE LEGISLATURE

The 2014 constitution established a unicameral, or one-house, legislative body, the Assembly of the Representatives of the People (ARP). This parliament consists of 217 representatives serving five-year terms, with members elected on party lists in 33 multimember constituencies. In the 2014 parliamentary elections, the secularist Nidaa Tounes party received a plurality of seats in the ARP.

THE JUDICIAL SYSTEM

The judiciary, or court system, is responsible for administrating justice. This branch operates independently of the other parts of government. In 2016, as required by the new constitution, the Supreme Judicial Council was established. This four-part body is charged with ensuring the independence of the judiciary and appointing Constitutional Court judges.

However, the new Tunisian constitution of 2014 called for the creation of a constitutional court of twelve members by the end of 2015; however, as of spring 2017, the court had not been appointed.

In addition to the regular courts—the Court of Cassation (high courts), appellate courts (courts of appeals), and courts of first instance (primary

THE CODE OF PERSONAL STATUS

The 2014 constitution provides for gender equality. Article 21 states, "All citizens, male and female, have equal rights and duties, and are equal before the law without any discrimination."

In this way, the constitution is in opposition to shariah law. This equality did not begin with this new constitution, however; it was made law in 1957 under the Code of Personal Status. This code altered the legal basis for the family and the status of women, not by rejecting Islamic values, but rather by rendering them more congruent with secular principles. To many traditionalist Muslims, however, any alteration is considered blasphemous.

In Tunisia, as in other countries, a patriarchal society is an important part of tradition. According to tradition, men are the heads of households—the decision makers and judges, hearing disputes between family members and deciding on punishments. Men inherit property, are educated to the highest affordable level, and take jobs outside of the home. Women are protected by men but are subordinate to them. The traditional social unit is the extended family, usually living in one house, with the head of the household being the oldest male. Property is held in common by the family. Men work together and expenses are divided equally. Women look after children until the age of six, when boys are turned over to the care of their fathers, who make all decisions concerning their education and discipline. Girls remain under the care of their mothers until marriage. Muslim men are allowed to have up to four wives, and they have the power to divorce a wife simply by saying, "I divorce thee," three times in front of male witnesses.

The Code of Personal Status changed all this. Polygamy was outlawed and divorce became a court's decision, not a man's personal one. In addition, now either marriage partner may petition for divorce. The legal age for marriage was set in 1964 at seventeen years for females and twenty for males. The mother was given the guardianship of all young children when divorce occurred, but the court had the power to appoint a guardian if a mother was deemed unfit. All women were encouraged to reach the highest educational and professional levels within their capability. They were given a choice and a voice when abortion and contraceptives were legalized and when they got the right to vote under the Code of Personal Status.

However, despite the constitutional assertion of gender equality, the Code does, in fact, discriminate against women when it comes to the inheritance of property. Essentially, male heirs inherit twice as much as female heirs.

trial courts)—there is a separate Constitutional Court. This body of twelve legal experts reviews new laws and treaties to make sure they align with the constitution. The president, the parliament, and the Supreme Judicial Council each appoint four members to this court. Those members serve for a single nine-year term.

LOCAL GOVERNMENT

Tunisia is divided into twenty-four governorates, called *wilayat*, (singular is *wilayah*), each named after its chief town.

The system of local governance is based on municipal, district-level, and regional elections. However, these elections have been repeatedly postponed, partly because of a lack of resources and partly because of debate as to whether members of the security forces should be allowed to participate. The government pledged the polls would be held in 2017; however the planned March elections of this year were also postponed.

INTERNET LINKS

http://www.aljazeera.com/indepth/features/2013/09/201394183325728267.html
"Who Killed Chokri Belaid?"takes a look at political assassinations in Tunisia in 2013.

https://www.constituteproject.org/constitution/Tunisia_2014.pdf
This is a transcript of Tunisia's 2014 constitution in English.

https://freedomhouse.org/report/freedom-world/2017/tunisia
Freedom House reviews the country's government annually, with regard to democracy and freedom.

http://www.pm.gov.tn/pm/content/?lang=en
This is the official portal for the government of Tunisia, in English.

ECONOMY

The Tunisian poet Aboul-Qacem Echebbi is pictured on the ten dinar banknote.

4

T HE 2011 REVOLUTION BROUGHT some good changes to Tunisia. However, the years since 2011 have been marked by slow economic growth and high unemployment, particularly among young people. Ironically, those same conditions were part of what provoked the revolution in the first place.

In the 1960s, the Tunisian government focused on expanding exports, attracting more foreign investment, and building up tourism. It also worked on improving education and infrastructure throughout the country. These policies successfully stimulated decades of 4—5 percent economic growth each year, which greatly improved living standards.

Zine el Abidine Ben Ali served as president from 1987—2011, during which time he continued these policies. However, cronyism and corruption in his administration began to negatively affect economic performance. The country's growing numbers of university graduates found it harder and harder to find jobs, and rising discontent simmered. These conditions contributed to the January 2011 overthrow of Ben Ali. The violence and uncertainty of the revolution itself naturally kept both tourists and foreign investors away, which led to a sharp decline in the economy.

Tunisia's government has been slow to turn this situation around. It needs to create stability in order to boost economic growth, and must find a solution to the high levels of youth unemployment. In this, Tunisia also faces a new challenge that it shares with much of the Arab

In 2016, the European Union granted Tunisia a two-year tax break on the import of olive oil. It provided this relief in response to Tunisia's recent economic woes, partially the result of terrorist attacks on its important tourism sector.

world—the rise of ISIS (the Islamic State, also known as ISIL and Daesh), a fundamentalist militant group. Successive terrorist attacks in Tunisia have certainly not helped the tourism sector. In fact, terror attacks have specifically targeted tourists for exactly that purpose. As of 2017, the United States and the United Kingdom, among other countries, have issued advisories against travel to Tunisia.

AGRICULTURE

Agriculture contributes about 10.1 percent to Tunisia's economic output. The agricultural sector provides most of Tunisia's own food and employs half of the nation's workforce. Cash crops include wheat, barley, grapes, olives, citrus fruit, and dates. Market produce such as tomatoes, sugar beets, potatoes, artichokes, fruit, and almonds have been added to diversify cultivation and increase income. Since Tunisia has an early growing season, its exports reach Europe ahead of the European season. Cotton is also grown to supply the textile industry, and esparto grass (a coarse grass used in the manufacture of paper) is grown on the plains.

A Tunisian worker harvests oranges at a farm in Menzel Bou Zelfa in the northeastern region of Nabul.

TUNISIA'S LIQUID GOLD

Olives have been an important crop in Tunisia for more than three thousand years. Most of these go into the production of olive oil. Sfax, the country's olive oil capital, exports most of this so-called Tunisian gold. Olive groves near Sfax stretch for up to 50 miles (80 km) inland from the coast.

In 2014–2015, Tunisia was the world's second-largest producer of olive oil, after Spain. That year, the nation's yield was estimated to be 280,000 to 300,000 tons (254,000 to 272,000 metric tons), a whopping 400 percent increase from the previous year's figure. That's way above average, which is 180,000 tons (163,000 t) of olive oil each year. (Sure enough, the yield for the subsequent season was a mere 100,000 tons (90,000 t), showing how changeable the industry can be.)

The olive tree, which is resistant to drought, is well adapted to Tunisia's climate. However, with climate change bringing hotter, drier condition to Tunisia, the outlook for the future may not be so rosy. Today, 80 percent of the country's eighty million olive trees are not irrigated and depend entirely on rainwater. By 2030, some analysts predict olive production could be cut in half. The World Resources Institute also predicts that by 2040, Tunisia will become one of the thirty-three most-water-stressed countries in the world.

Only a small percentage of Tunisia's olive oil is consumed at home. About 80 percent of it is exported, mostly to Europe, where it is blended with other oils under a large variety of brand names. Olive oils from Italy and Spain have long been promoted as superior, and bottles claiming to contain 100 percent Italian olive oil, for example, can fetch higher prices. Weary of seeing its own liquid gold disappear anonymously into blends, the Tunisian olive industry is now trying to promote its home-grown oil as an upscale brand. In 2017, Tunisia won its first Gold Award at the New York International Olive Oil Competition, a hopeful sign for the nation's future.

On the island of Djerba, fishing boats are piled high with nets.

Despite the great dry areas in the south of the country, about half of Tunisia is classified as productive pasture and forest. The government has undertaken irrigation and soil conservation projects to improve production. To raise funds for the agricultural sector, the government created the Agricultural Investment Promotion Agency and the National Agricultural Development Bank. At test farms, researchers experiment to try to improve the quality and variety of crops. A higher institute of agricultural research and instruction links farmers and researchers. New methods of cultivation and research results are made known to the farmers, and farmers' concerns are brought to the researchers to evaluate.

FISHING

For a country with such a long coast line, it's not surprising that commercial fishing is an extremely important part of the Tunisian economy. Some 70—75 percent of the nation's fishing activity takes place on the central eastern coast.

Aquaculture is a growing industry, which is being encouraged in order to relieve pressure on wild catch fish stocks. Farmed seabass and seabream make up the largest part of Tunisia's production. Most aquaculture production is in the Monastir governorate, along Tunisia's eastern shore. Bluefin tuna farming is a relatively new endeavor, with the first company starting out in 2003; by 2016, there were five private companies in that sector. Mussels, oysters, and other shellfish are also being farmed.

FORESTRY

The main export in the Tunisian forestry sector is cork, which grows in abundance in the forested northwest. The bark of cork oak is first stripped off when the tree is twenty years old. The first layer is rough and is shredded for use in products such as floor tiles and placemats. Every ten years, bark is removed, the rough surface is scraped, and the remaining layer is flattened and dried before further processing as cork stoppers or other products.

MINING

Tunisia is the world's fifth-largest producer of phosphate, with 5 percent of the world's reserves. Phosphate is an inorganic salt of phosphoric acid; a compound commonly found in phosphate rocks. It is used in many applications, particularly in chemical fertilizers. Phosphates account for nearly 45 percent the country's export earnings.

Oil exploration in Tunisia began in 1956 after reserves were found in Algeria. In 2017, Tunisia was producing 51,000 barrels of oil per day, down from its highest level of 95,000 in 1994. Like other sectors of the economy, both the phosphate and oil industries went into decline after the 2011 revolution. Worker strikes against poor working conditions played a role as well.

In May 2017, following another wave of protests over unemployment and worsening economic conditions, President Beji Caid Essebsi ordered the army to protect the mines. It was the first time Tunisian troops had been deployed to guard industrial facilities—including phosphate, gas and oil production facilities—that are key to the national economy.

INDUSTRY

Manufacturing makes up roughly 28.3 percent of Tunisia's gross domestic product (GDP) and employs about 33.2 percent of the workforce. Heavy industry, developed with the help of foreign investments, focuses on mineral refining. Oil refineries, chemical plants, iron and steelworks, and cement production have grown around the sites of deposits. Auto assembly plants mainly put together trucks and tractors.

Tunisia's light industries include food processing (flour milling, food canning, sugar refining, and olive oil processing), textile and leather production, and paper and wood processing. Textiles and clothing have become increasingly important export earners over the last twenty years.

The Bardo National Museum in Tunis is one of Africa's largest and most important museums. It once attracted hundreds of thousands of visitors each year, 90 percent of them foreign tourists. At midday, on March 18, 2015, two young Tunisian men began shooting at foreign vacationers who were disembarking a tour bus to enter the museum. The shooters pursued the frightened people into the building and continued shooting. They held more than one hundred people hostage, and many others hid. The siege lasted three hours, leaving twenty-one people dead and forty-seven injured, including victims from Japan, Italy, France, Australia, Colombia, Poland, and Spain. Security forces killed the two gunmen, and searched for a reported third terrorist.

ISIS, the Islamic State terror network, responded with glee to the account and quickly claimed responsibility. In the months that followed, authorities arrested some twenty people on suspicion of direct or indirect involvement of the massacre.

Three months after the Bardo attack, on June 26, terrorists staged another attack on tourists. This time, a single gunman opened fire on vacationers at the popular beach resort of Port El Kantaoui, just north of Sousse. He killed thirty-eight people on the beach and in the elegant Hotel Rui Imperial Marhana, including thirty British victims. The twenty-three-year-old Tunisian gunman was shot dead shortly afterward by police. Once again, ISIS claimed responsibility. The supposed mastermind of both the Bardo and Sousse attacks, Chamseddine al-Sandi, remains at large, possibly in Libya.

European clothing firms have subcontracted work to Tunisian factories because of the low wages and high skills of the labor force. Another burgeoning industry is electronics. Cooperative-run small cottage industries produce traditional crafts. Mostly handmade using antique tools, these crafts have a long history in Tunisia.

TOURISM

Tourism has been a very important source of revenue for Tunisia, attracting nearly seven million visitors per year. It accounts for 8 percent of Tunisia's GDP and is a key source of foreign currency and jobs.

Prior to 2011, Tunisia was a popular destination for many European vacationers, who flocked to its sunny beaches, ancient ruins, and exotic desert locales. For them, Tunisia was a nearby, safe, and affordable destination. Coastal cities like Sousse and Hammamet catered to this tourist crowd, attracting visitors from France, Germany, Italy, and Britain.

The number of visitors dropped from 6.9 million in 2010 to 4.8 million in 2011. Things were just starting to pick up again when, in 2015, two major terrorist attacks occurred. In the aftermath, nearly two hundred major Tunisian hotels shut down due to loss of business. By 2017, officials from the Tourism Ministry said hotel booking rates for the summer were rising, especially with bargain packages attracting visitors from Russia.

Tourists visit the ruins of a Roman temple in Dougga, a UNESCO World Heritage Site in northern Tunisia.

INTERNET LINKS

http://africa-me.com/a-great-season-for-tunisias-olive-oil
This article provides a good look at Tunisia's olive oil industry.

https://www.alaraby.co.uk/english/comment/2016/5/5/terrorism-and-tourism-in-tunisia
Terrorism's affect on Tunisia's tourism industry is the subject of this article.

https://www.thenational.ae/world/tunisia-s-olive-farming-under-threat-1.42543
This article looks at the damage that climate change poses to Tunisia's olive industry.

ENVIRONMENT

A camel sporting a richly decorated blanket walks on a Tunisian beach.

5

GIVEN ITS SMALL SIZE, TUNISIA IS A biologically diverse country, with lush oak forests in the north contrasting with a dry Saharan landscape just a few hundred miles to the south. In Tunisia today the main environmental threats to this diversity are desertification and land erosion in the green north and center, industrial pollution in the cities, limited water resources, and the disposal of human and industrial waste. A number of mammal and bird species are also endangered, as are some types of plants. Most of these problems are due to rapid economic development—an increase in farming, industrial expansion, and the spread of towns and cities.

The Tunisian government takes its environmental responsibilities seriously and has sought to introduce policies that preserve and protect the country's natural resources without slowing economic growth. Tunisia's Ministry of the Environment and Sustainable Development coordinates a number of government agencies that are responsible for

In January 2014, Tunisia became the third country in the world (after Ecuador and the Dominican Republic) to adopt a legal commitment to climate change. Article 45 of the new constitution reads, "The state shall guarantee the right to a sound and balanced environment and contribute to a sound climate. The state shall provide the necessary means to eliminate environmental pollution."

Tunisia stands to be seriously affected by climate change, but there's not a great deal it can do about it. A 2015 report issued by the country's Department of the Environment and Sustainable Development said Tunisia "is considered among the most exposed Mediterranean countries in terms of climate change." The risk of rising temperatures and sea levels, droughts, and floods, it warned, "translate into a profound environmental and socioeconomic vulnerability."

Increased drought, for example, is already threatening the nation's crucial olive industry, which employs about 400,000 people. And

Candles arranged to read 'Tunisia' mark an Earth Hour demonstration in Tunis as people gather to support protecting the planet.

although Tunisia signed onto the Paris climate accord, pledging to reduce its carbon dioxide (CO_2) emissions by 41 percent by 2030, its role in the global effort will make little difference—Tunisia contributes less than 0.07 percent of the world's total CO_2 emissions. (CO_2 is one of several key so-called greenhouse gases emitted by human activities which are affecting the atmosphere in a way that is causing climate change. CO_2 comes mostly from the use of fossil fuels and is the greatest contributor to the greenhouse effect.)

Like other small countries, Tunisia suffers the effects of climate change, but has little influence over the big players. The top three greenhouse gas emitters—China, the European Union, and the United States—contribute more than half of total global emissions, while the bottom one hundred countries, which includes Tunisia, only account for 3.5 percent.

protecting the environment, improving sanitation, developing renewable energies, and protecting the coastline and local marine life. On the whole, Tunisia has been successful in reducing damage to the environment, with a record that is better than that of most other African and Arab countries.

LAND DEGRADATION

Deforestation, land erosion, and desertification go hand-in-hand, and represent some of Tunisia's most pressing environmental problems today. The misuse of fertile lands and the destruction of forests, coupled with the affects of climate change, cause land erosion and degradation that, in turn, transform green regions into desert—a process called desertification. This is a global trend, affecting roughly one-third of the world's land surface, but in Tunisia it threatens almost three-quarters of the country's land.

According to the U.N. Convention to Combat Desertification, Tunisia is losing about 100,000 acres (40,500 hectares) of land every year to erosion. Land erosion, if left unchecked, can drastically reduce the number of species

The old village of Zaafrane, near Douz, is literally being buried by the encroaching desert.

of animals and plants that are able to survive in the new conditions. The encroaching desert has even overtaken some towns and forced people to move.

In the north and central part of the country, over 7.4 million acres (3 million ha) of land are eroding mainly because of farming practices, while in the south, 17.3 million acres (7 million ha) of land are being turned into desert by wind erosion and a creeping sand invasion from the Sahara. Located on the edge of the Sahara Desert, the region of Jeffara in the southeast of Tunisia, near the Libyan border, is especially affected. The soil in this area is weak and has become damaged as more and more land has been used for farming.

The government has tried to encourage the development of industries other than farming, so that there will be less strain on the water resources and soil of the region. The government has also tried to combat these problems through soil and water conservation programs and by developing "green belts"—areas planted with grass and trees—around newly built areas of towns and cities.

WATER RESOURCES

Like all other North African countries, Tunisia's water supply is affected by changes in climate, especially variations in rainfall. The fertile north of the country gets more than ten times as much rainfall as the dry, sub-Saharan south, although in recent years rainfall has been very unpredictable, with occasional periods of drought being followed by heavy floods.

Due to increasing droughts, mismanaged water resources, and growing population, Tunisia faces severe water shortage problems, particularly in the summer. The quality of water varies throughout the country and does not meet potable standards in some regions.

More than 80 percent of the country's water is used for farming. This has stretched local water supplies from rivers and underground springs thin, as modern farming techniques and growing towns use up more water at a faster rate. The same water supplies are used for drinking, household waste, irrigation, and feeding farm animals. Olive groves and fruit trees in particular need lots of water, and these crops are heavily farmed today in north and central Tunisia.

The national water utility operates sixteen water treatment plants and eleven desalination plants throughout the country. They serve about 84 percent of the population, but only 47.5 percent in rural areas. In farming regions, agricultural development cooperatives use both shallow and deep wells and tap into the utility's pumping stations and distribution networks. Aquifer levels are declining at an alarming rate.

In July 2017, the reservoir bed of Tunisia's El-Haouareb dam is totally dry. Located near Kairouan, the region was facing acute water shortages due to drought conditions.

WASTE MANAGEMENT

Tunisia has one of the best records for waste management among North African and Middle Eastern countries. Since the late 1990s, Tunisia has benefited from the advice and expertise of waste management companies in developed countries, especially Japan.

Urban waste is collected and taken to government dumping grounds. Up until the 1990s, industrial and medical waste—such as used needles, toxic substances, and human waste—was not separated out before collection, and was often disposed of along with normal household refuse. However,

Gabes, Tunisia, looks like paradise. Located on Tunisia's southeastern coast on the Mediterranean Sea, the city has white sand beaches and green palm trees. But Gabes is also a major industrial hub and the center of the phosphate processing industry.

Phosphate is a necessary plant nutrient found in the earth, often in rock deposits. Phosphate rock is mined primarily for the production of fertilizers. However, the bright yellow rock itself is not that useful to plants because the phosphorus in this form is not very soluble—that is, it doesn't mix with water into a material the plant can absorb. Treating phosphate rock with sulfuric acid produces phosphoric acid, which is water-soluble, and therefore is the material used in most phosphate fertilizers.

In 2017, local men shout anti-government slogans during a protest against the pollution caused by factories in the Gabes region.

The huge phosphate industry accounts for 30 percent of Tunisia's economy, and employs more than three thousand people. In the early 1970s, the Tunisian Chemical Group built a phosphate-refining plant in the Gabes region to make fertilizers and preservatives for export. Raw phosphate from mines in Gafsa and other towns in Tunisia's interior is processed in Gabes, and from there, shipped to global markets.

The production process dumps a radioactive waste product called phosphogypsum in the Gulf of Gabes—some 13,000 tons (11,800 tonnes) a day. (Some environmental groups claim the true amount is much higher.) This dangerous pollutant has poisoned the waters, killed off marine life, and turned coastal stretches into an industrial wasteland. Today, locals call the Gabes beach Chott al-Mout, *or "The Death Shore."*

The people of Gabes are suffering as well. The plant releases toxic gases into the air, causing a stench to hang over the city. Mystery illnesses plague the population, and the incidence of asthma, skin disorders, cancers, and birth defects are much higher than normal—in fact, Gabes has Tunisia's highest rate of cancer.

Although environmental groups raise awareness and residents protest, industry officials claim they cannot afford to fix the pollution problem. The Tunisian government, likewise, lacks the money and power to confront such a formidable sector of the national economy.

the government has built more than a dozen sanitary landfills. About 80 percent all refuse is now properly disposed of, which is a big improvement. According to the government, 4 percent of municipal solid waste is recycled, while 70 percent is dumped in controlled landfills, 21 percent in non-controlled landfills, and 5 percent is composted. However, many municipal landfills are unsatisfactory by today's standards.

In Djerba, color-coded trash bins encourage garbage sorting and recycling.

INDUSTRIAL POLLUTION

Air pollution is a serious threat to the environment in Tunisia, especially in big industrial cities such as Tunis, Sfax, Sousse, and Gabes. Trucks and cars use one-third of the country's energy resources—mostly petroleum—and cause most of the country's air pollution. The largest industrial polluters are cement factories, paper mills, chemical industries, and oil refineries, whose thermoelectric power releases toxic gases into the air.

PROTECTED PARKS AND WETLANDS

There are eight protected national parks and nature reserves in Tunisia. The best known are the Ichkuel National Park, Chaambi National Park, Zembra Island Nature Reserve, El Feija National Park, Bou Hedma National Park, and Hadaj National Park. There are also 16 smaller nature reserves that are protected under Tunisian law. These include the bat caves at El Haouaria and the Kchem El Kelb reserve for gazelles.

Tunisia's wetlands are found mostly in the north of the country. These stretch over 2.5 million acres (1 million ha) and include seven major sea and coastal lakes and more than thirty smaller salt lakes. Conservationists

CONSERVATION IN ICHKEUL NATIONAL PARK

One of Tunisia's UNESCO World Heritage sites is Ichkeul National Park. The 23-square-mile (60 sq km) park is dominated by Lake Ichkeul. This freshwater lake is linked by a narrow channel to the nearby saltwater Lake Bizerte. Ichkeul is one of the rarest types of lakes in the world, with fresh water during the rainy winter months and salt water during the drier summer months. This unique ecosystem has been protected as a national park since 1996. The park is home to five hundred plant species and two hundred species of birds. Hunting, fishing, and grazing animals are illegal within the park boundaries. The park is also home to important animal fossils.

For many centuries the lake has been North Africa's main wintering ground for hundreds of thousands of birds migrating from Europe. The birds that nest among the reed beds of the lake include ducks, greylag geese, wading birds—such as avocets and Kentish plovers—and numerous types of herons and egrets. White storks and flamingos nest around the park and feed in the lake. The park is also home to a local species of otter, which has been hunted over the years for its meat and is now extremely rare.

In the 1990s, dams on the rivers that feed the lake, coupled with low rainfall, caused salt water from Lake Bizerte to flow back into Lake Ichkuel. This killed off some water plants and reed beds on which the lake's delicate ecosystem depends. The change severely affected some of the migrating bird species that fed and nested in the reed beds. The purple heron, purple gallinule, and great reed warbler became very rare. Conservationists estimate that if freshwater levels in the lake continued to decline, the lake might eventually become a seawater lagoon. Because of this, the park was added to UNESCO's World Heritage in Danger list in 1996. In response, the Tunisian government added a series of locks to control the levels of fresh water in the lake, and has had some success in preserving the lake's delicate ecological balance. The park was subsequently removed from the Danger List in 2006.

estimate that the wetlands attract up to half a million birds migrating from Europe each year, and also support a local population of 350,000 birds. More than half of all ducks in North Africa, as well as 25,000 flamingos, migrate to Tunisia, and the wetlands support at least thirty species of sandpipers.

In recent years the country's wetlands have been threatened by industrial pollution, unplanned building development, and a rapid increase in farming. Scientists estimate that Tunisia has lost more than a quarter of its wetlands in the last century, with building causing the destruction of 8,154 acres (3,300 ha) each year.

INTERNET LINKS

http://www.al-monitor.com/pulse/politics/2014/08/tunisia-ecology-environment-pollution.html
This article decries the average Tunisian's lack of environmental awareness.

http://www.dw.com/en/the-quiet-environmental-disaster-in-tunisia/a-16796561
This article reveals the severe environmental problem caused by industrial pollution in the city of Gabes.

http://www.environnement.gov.tn
This official website of Tunisia's Ministry of the Environment and Sustainable Development offers an English version available by clicking in the upper right hand corner.

http://whc.unesco.org/en/list/8
This is the World Heritage listing for Ichkeul National Park.

TUNISIANS

6

ALMOST EVERYONE IN TUNISIA IS A Sunni Muslim, and almost everyone is Arab. This is a very homogeneous society, but that is not to say that everyone is the same. There are rich, business-suited, pro-Western Tunisians as well as poor, robed, uneducated herders who are suspicious of Western values and who barely survive off the land.

On October 9, 2015, the Tunisian National Dialogue Quartet was awarded the 2015 Nobel Peace Prize. The quartet is a group of four organizations that came together in the summer of 2013 to build a pluralistic democracy in Tunisia following the 2011 revolution. Those organizations were the Tunisian General Labour Union, the Tunisian Confederation of Industry, the Tunisian Human Rights League, and the Tunisian Order of Lawyers.

A small boy carries trinkets to sell to tourists at a popular stop in the Sahara Desert.

A bustling marketplace in Tozeur attracts people from nearby villages.

Some people are politically and religiously progressive, while others are extremely conservative. And, being an African nation of people who descend from Arab, Berber, Mediterranean, European, and sub-Saharan peoples, physical features also vary—although no official statistics exist, some 15 percent of Tunisians could be said to be black, while the rest identify as white. That's why, in large public gatherings, Tunisians can appear to be a diverse people.

POPULATION STATISTICS

In 2016 the population of Tunisia was about 11,134,600. The overwhelming majority of people live in the northern half of the country, while the desert south is sparsely populated. In the Saharan region, there are as few as nine people per square mile (five per square km). About 66.8 percent of the population lives in urban centers (up from just 33 percent in 1956), which make up 20 percent of the land. (In Tunis alone, there are nearly two million people.) The remaining people, mainly farmers and herders, live in the northeast, the Sahel, the plains, and the Saharan region.

Since gaining independence in 1957, improved public health care has increased the average life expectancy in Tunisia from fifty to approximately seventy-six years. Infant mortality is 21.6 per 1,000 births. There are publicly and privately financed programs to assist poor and disadvantaged people.

The adult literacy rate, meaning the percentage of people over age fifteen who can read and write, in 2015 was 81.8 percent, with some gender difference— men, 89.6 percent; women, 74.2 percent). These figures continue to rise. Education is highly prized and is seen as the only way out of poverty and into a higher social class.

ETHNIC GROUPS

The racial blend of Tunisians is the result of centuries of history—the original Berber people mixing with Phoenicians, Romans, Spaniards, Arabs, and the French. There are also very small groups of Europeans, Africans, Jews, and Spaniards.

ARAB-BERBERS The Arabs came to Tunisia in the seventh century with the intention of conquering the Berbers and spreading Islam. Many Arabs settled down and married Berbers, spreading the Arab language and culture, and creating a new Maghreb identity. Arabization was complete by the eleventh century, following the invasion of a few thousand Beni Hillal Bedouin, who converted a few million Berbers to Islam. The Arabs were generally of slender build with dark hair, eyes, and skin.

BERBERS Now only 2 percent of the population, much less than in Algeria or Morocco, today's Berbers are the descendants of those who retained their identity by evading successive groups of invaders. The majority settled in the Atlas Mountains, the Sahara, and on Djerba Island, where they followed a nomadic life that was introduced by the Beni Hillal Bedouin tribes. Even today

A Berber family poses in the desert village of Chenini, one of the oldest Berber abodes in Tunisia.

many Berbers raise herds of sheep and goats and live in caves or mud-walled or underground homes in Matmata, Medenine, and Tataouine, all towns in the Ksour region.

Young, single Berber men leave their homes for cities and even emigrate to France and Libya in search of work and higher wages to send home. They usually return to Tunisia to look for a wife. Older people populate Berber villages, many of whom are women who struggle to eke out a living by weaving carpets.

The Berbers are the first known inhabitants of the Maghreb, who probably lived there for thousands of years before the arrival of the Phoenicians. Their origin is mysterious. They might have come from a combination of peoples—Libyan, Egyptian, Persian, Phoenician, Italian, and Iberian. Generally stocky in build, with light hair and blue eyes, Berbers are independent and individualistic.

Some scholars believe that *Berber* is not the original name of these people, because it is a derogatory word that comes from the Greek *barabaroi* or the Arabian *brabra*, used to describe strangers whose language is unintelligible.

AFRICANS Descendants of sub-Saharan Africans who were brought to Tunisia as domestic slaves and concubines form this minority group. They have affected the population only slightly.

SPANISH Muslims fled from Spain for a few hundred years, starting in the thirteenth century when the Spanish fought to get their territory back from the Ottoman Turks. In Tunisia they intermarried with the local people and left a social and cultural impact on the coastal society.

JEWS Jews have been present in Tunisia for almost two thousand years, and today they are mostly merchants and skilled craftspeople. The population of Jews was sufficiently large before independence to require the establishment of rabbinical courts to settle their legal affairs based on religious principles. Several thousand Jews left Tunisia gradually, over two decades, after World War II. The first Jews arrived in Tunisia after the Roman emperor Titus burned Jerusalem. Others came when the Christian king Philip III expelled them from Spain. The Jews who came in the early twentieth century were middle-class traders from Europe. Tensions in the Middle East since independence has led to demonstrations against the Jews of Tunisia. Demonstrations and the vandalism of synagogues have given rise to feelings of insecurity among the Jews.

EUROPEANS When the French protectorate was established, French and Italians flooded into Tunisia. Generally the French were the wealthy elite, while the Italians were mostly working-class people from southern Italy, particularly Sicily. After independence, in the late 1950s and 1960s, the Europeans left Tunisia in large numbers. The French, especially, left their mark on Tunisia in the architecture, food, language, tree-lined avenues, sidewalk cafés, and Western clothing, which is worn everywhere. Today small European communities can be found in Tunis and Bizerte.

EMIGRATION

The urban centers generally have better job opportunities and facilities such as schools and hospitals. Consequently there has been a constant movement of people from rural to urban centers. As the nomadic way of life dies out in the desert and mountain regions, the government has tried resettling nomads and semi-nomads in permanent villages and teaching them to grow crops for export.

However, unemployment has long prompted Tunisians to go abroad for work. In 2012, more than 1.2 million people (out of a population of 11 million) were living and working outside the country. Indeed, the government encouraged it. The money emigrants sent home stimulated the economy, while the emigration of workers relieved pressure on Tunisia's domestic unemployment. Historic connections with France and Italy made those countries popular emigration destinations.

The social upheaval around the time of the 2011 revolution caused a spike in emigration, leading up to 25,000 migrants to leave Tunisia illegally. But as the new government introduced reforms, including the new constitution in 2014, the trend slowed. Whereas emigrants used to be primarily semi- and unskilled laborers, the new emigration pattern includes university graduates who cannot find professional employment at home.

CLASS STRUCTURE AND ATTITUDES

The Tunisian government estimates that 75 to 80 percent of Tunisians are middle-class, a consequence of steadily rising living standards over the last twenty years. The upper-middle class of Tunisia—the economic and political elite—is made up of the old aristocratic families, Western-educated civil servants, political leaders, prominent businesspeople, and large landowners. The lower-middle class—a quickly growing group—consists of low-level civil servants, schoolteachers, small business owners, skilled service and industrial workers, and independent farmers. The working class is made

Men harvest dates in southwest Tunisia.

up of subsistence farmers and agricultural workers. The day laborers, unemployed, and underemployed found in rural areas and shantytowns near urban centers belong to Tunisia's lowest social class.

There is a fundamental difference in attitude between people in fertile northern and coastal Tunisia and those in the more remote central and southern parts. In the fertile areas people are richer and are more in control of their lives. They value education, political leadership, commercial success, and wealth. They have a greater sense of security and are aware of their right to property. In the arid regions people have a sense of helplessness and turn to religion in times of crisis, since extremes of climate can affect their livelihood.

Education is of great importance to most Tunisians, but it is the tie that binds the elite together, who are mainly educated at French secondary schools. For higher education many go abroad or to the University of Tunis. The working and lower classes are more attuned to the Arab world and Islam, and are less receptive to Western influences. These people make up the majority of the population, and the government depends on them for stability. The government has had to constantly balance the needs of a developing economy while maintaining its Islamic identity. For example, the government publicly condemned the United States—led invasion and occupation of Iraq in 2003 for the sake of Islamic unity while at the same time maintaining its policy of building closer economic ties with the United States and the European Union. Farmers and nomads in the rural areas are generally suspicious of urban life.

In general Tunisians are warm and generous people. They have a civic spirit and very readily lend a hand without thought of reward. Foreigners are pleasantly surprised when Tunisians go out of their way to help them. It is also common to see Tunisians giving alms to the less fortunate.

DRESS

As in most other Islamic countries, traditional Tunisian clothes mostly include loose-fitting robes that cover the arms, legs, and head. In cities people dress in both Western and traditional clothes, but those who wear

A man dressed in typical Tunisian style walks on Avenue Habib Bourguiba in Tunis.

Western clothes observe the basic rule of modesty. Many Western-educated and young Tunisians, as well as businesspeople, prefer Western attire, sometimes complemented with a traditional Tunisian garment such as a hat or a loose robe worn as an outer garment when going outdoors.

Even those people who usually wear Western clothing will wear traditional attire for special occasions, such as weddings. The clothing for such ceremonies is often richly embroidered.

The *chehias* (shair-HI-ah)—hats—that Tunisian men wear are tall and brimless. They can be round or flat-topped, brown or red. The color indicates the area the men come from. The *djellaba* is a loose long-sleeved robe that usually includes a baggy hood. The *jebba* is a similar garment, more of a tunic worn with baggy trouser and sometimes a vest. In the desert, men wear a length of fabric tied around their heads like a turban and an extremely loose tunic that can be wrapped around their heads and bodies when they need to protect themselves from the cold, heat, wind, or dust.

Traditional women line their eyes with black kohl, while Berber women have blue dots tattooed on their forehead, nose, and chin. Traditional attire for women is the *sefsari (or sefseri)* and *haik*, a long tunic and a large sheet that can be pulled over the head and the corners clenched by the teeth. The haik plays double role as a veil and as a wrap that can be used to carry packages or babies.

Women's hands are commonly painted with henna, a natural brown dye, for special occasions such as weddings. Jewelry made of copper, brass, silver, and gold are frequently worn. Traditionally, the jewelry that a single woman wore was a sign of her family's wealth, advertising her eligibility. Brides still wear abundant amounts of gold jewelry today. Turquoise (the French word for "Turkish blue," a color favored by the Turks for decorative tiles) and amber are popular because they are believed to have protective powers.

Two Tunisian women in the desert region are dressed in traditional clothing.

INTERNET LINKS

http://www.aljazeera.com/programmes/peopleandpower/2016/03/tunisia-dirty-secret-160316153815980.html
This article discusses the rarely discussed problem of racism in Tunisia.

http://www.ins.tn/en/front
Tunisia's National Institute of Statistics offers up to dates information on demographics and other topics.

https://www.newsecuritybeat.org/2011/01/tunisias-shot-at-democracy-what-demographics-and-recent-history-tell-us
Though it dates from 2011, this article makes interesting points about the correlation between demographics and democracy.

http://www.worldatlas.com/webimage/countrys/africa/tunisia/tnfamous.htm
This site provides a long list of prominent Tunisians.

LIFESTYLE

Tataouine in southern Tunisia is known for its cave dwellings.

7

UNISIANS ARE STILL EMERGING from the revolutionary events of 2011. It's a time of transition and change that affects daily life. Although Tunisia was the only country to came through the Arab Spring successfully, with a relatively peaceful conversion to democracy, there is apprehension among ordinary people about the future holds. Political rights and civil liberties are less restrictive than before, but certain freedoms, such as the ability to criticize Islam, the government, or the army, remain curtailed. On the other hand, some people complain of feeling less secure now that the police presence is less noticeable.

In the uncertain times that followed the revolution, tens of thousands of Tunisians—particularly young people—migrated illegally to Italy and France, adding to the rush of neighboring Libyans fleeing the civil war in that country.

Although women enjoy some of the same rights as men, differences do remain. For example, a Tunisian man is allowed to marry a foreign woman, regardless of her religion, with no legal requirements. However, a Tunisian woman is only allowed to marry a foreign non-Muslim man as long as the man converts to Islam. That process can take more than three months.

HOUSING

Most people live in urban areas in the north of the country, where nearly everyone has access to electricity, drinking water, and sanitary facilities. Tunisians mostly live in traditional, Mediterranean-style stone houses and villas. Although not very popular, high-rise living helps to maximize the limited land space in major cities.

A street scene in modern Tunis shows some of the residential building styles.

IN THE CITIES AND TOWNS
The movement of large numbers of people from rural areas to the cities in search of work led to the growth of squatter villages, or *gourbvilles*, just outside the cities. A green belt is being established around urban centers to improve air quality and to deter the formation of squatter villages. Trade unions provide housing for members, and needy homeowners can apply for help from the national housing fund. The government controls rent prices to keep them affordable.

Traditional homes vary widely, but, in general, many homes are small and line narrow streets, facing one another. The exterior walls of the houses are painted a single color. Although doors may be painted in different colors, blue is favored. Homes usually have three stories, with access from the third story to a flat, livable roof. Rarely are there windows in the exterior walls of Tunisian houses, but courtyards, sometimes with fountains and gardens, are often hidden behind these walls.

IN THE COUNTRYSIDE
Farmhouses are crudely made and are usually whitewashed. A low wall surrounds the house to keep out stray animals and windblown sand. Unusual loaf-shaped roofs, which are made entirely of bricks, allow air to circulate more efficiently inside, keeping the house cool in summer and warm in winter.

Furnishings are meager and basic. The oven is a brick hole in the wall and one charcoal burner serves as the stove. There is no refrigeration. Carpets are stored folded and then spread out when they are needed on dirt or stone floors—people sit, sleep, eat, and entertain on carpets.

In some places, water is collected from a communal well that is generally some distance away, so frequent trips must be made to keep rural homes supplied with water for cooking, cleaning, and drinking.

IN THE SOUTH AND DESERT AREAS The Tunisian south has some of the most unusual homes, which are occupied by mountain dwellers and nomads. These creative homes have existed for centuries, safeguarding people from the extremes of heat and cold, sand, wind, and wild animals.

Nomads carry their tented homes with them on the backs of camels. Bedouin tents are usually made of sacking that is woven and sewn together by the women. Rugs and blankets complete the homes' furnishings. These broad and low tents house entire families.

Underground dwellings called troglodyte homes, located near Matmata, Médenine, and Chenini, are a major tourist attraction. These Berber villages look like the surface of the moon, with craters emitting spirals of smoke. Their appearance is so strange that Steven Spielberg filmed *Raiders of the Lost Ark* and *Star Wars* in Matmata.

Troglodyte homes have open courtyards. Rooms, usually four in each home—one each for eating, sleeping, stabling, and storage—radiate out from the courtyard. The storage room holds necessities such as grain, olives, and animal fodder that can be restocked through a narrow pipe that leads to the outside through the ceiling. A tunnel, lined with places for storing tools and other items, connects the various rooms. A gently inclined entrance tunnel, big enough to lead a large animal through, connects the surface with the underground home. A few larger troglodyte homes in Matmata have been converted into hotels.

Farming in the desert climate is difficult, and it's possible to have only one good grain crop every few years. In earlier times, it was therefore vital to defend the village granary—called the *ghorfa* (GHOR-fa), Arabic for "room,"

In Matmata, some indigenous people still live underground, in troglodyte homes.

or *ksar* (SAHR), Arabic for "fortress"—from attack. *Ksars* and *ghorfas* are traditional mud and stone buildings. They were built on flat ridges or in sheltered valleys that were difficult for strangers to penetrate without being seen from lookout posts. The buildings have several rooms, built side-by-side and piled up to five or six levels high. Linked by interior or exterior stairs, they were built for defense against Arab troops. Grain is now stored closer to the fields, and these old buildings have been converted into homes.

EDUCATION

Most schools in Tunisia are government schools, and private schools (mostly Islamic and Catholic) are subject to government regulation. The curricula apply to all schools to ensure uniformity. A Ministry of National Education formulates and implements educational policy and supervises the standard of teaching and of facilities in primary and secondary schools. The Ministry of Higher Education and Scientific Research oversees higher education.

In 2012, about 6.3 percent of the government's annual budget was spent on education. Public education is provided free of charge from primary to university level, is compulsory for all children until the age of sixteen, and is made available to all Tunisians, regardless of gender, class, or ethnic background.

The educational system has three levels: primary school (which lasts six years), secondary school (three years), and university (four years) or vocational training (three years). Primary and secondary schools are open six days a week for nine months of the year. Instruction is in Arabic in the early primary school years, then in French in the later years. Nearly all children attend primary school, and about 76 percent continue through upper secondary school. At the secondary level, girls make up a slightly higher percentage of the student population than boys.

Tunisia's first university after independence, the University of Tunis, was opened in 1960, and for many years it was the only place of higher education in the country. However, both the Bourguiba and the Ben Ali governments were highly committed to improving the training and education of Tunisians. By 2006 there were thirteen public universities in Tunisia—up from just six in 2000—with 365,000 students enrolled full-time. There are also numerous private universities and other institutions of higher learning.

HEALTH AND SOCIAL SECURITY

In the early 1960s the government introduced a welfare program called the National Social Security Fund, to which employers and employees make contributions. The fund provides benefits for the sick and disabled, as well as for maternity, family allowances, life insurance, and old age. Social Security care for the aged, orphaned, and needy is deemed the responsibility of regional committees.

The government started a family planning program in 1964, the first of its kind in Africa. By 2006, the birthrate had dropped from 7 to 1.7 children per woman in Tunisia. By 2016, it had rebounded slightly to 1.98 children per woman.

WOMEN

Women in Tunisia are relatively free and independent compared with those in the other North African and Middle Eastern Islamic states. Habib Bourguiba, the first president, liberated women from subordination to men by creating the Code of Personal Status. Women are encouraged to enter all levels of education and professional life. Their civil rights respecting ownership of property, inheritance, custody of children, and divorce are equal to those of men.

POLITICAL RIGHTS Women have the right to vote. In 1956 the National Union of Tunisian Women was formed to voice women's problems and aspirations, and to promote female participation in the country's social and political life. Women's concerns regarding health, literacy, employment, and family planning are heard through this organization, which also helps women cope better personally and professionally by providing courses in topics such as literacy, civics, hygiene, family planning, and sewing.

In general, upper- and middle-class women are more daring in experimenting with their liberty than lower-class and rural women are. Today women work not only as teachers, seamstresses, and factory or agricultural workers, but also as lawyers, doctors, politicians, and civil servants.

RITES OF PASSAGE

Most life-cycle celebrations in Tunisia, regardless of religion, are practiced with a mixture of folklore and rituals. Belief in the evil eye and in djinns (evil spirits) is widespread and very much a part of all celebrations. Since 98 percent of the population is Muslim, the main life events are observed according to Islamic belief.

BIRTH Seven days after the birth of a child, amulets adorned with fish, coins, or teeth are worn by the child to protect it from evil forces. These amulets are believed to bring good luck.

CIRCUMCISION Between the ages of five and seven years, a boy makes his first visit to the mosque, where he is circumcised by a doctor or a barber (barbers have traditionally performed the circumcision ceremony).

At the precise moment of circumcision, other children break a jar of candy to keep the evil spirits, or djinns, from entering the boy's body through the wound.

WEDDINGS Marriage in Tunisia today requires the consent of the woman,

A young woman in the Tataouine region wears traditional Berber wedding attire.

who has to be at least seventeen years old. Polygamy is illegal, and women can initiate divorce proceedings that now must go through a civil court. These legally enforced changes make men socially and psychologically more committed to a marriage contract. Many couples these days protect their interests by having legal documents drawn up stating the terms of marriage and divorce, including the settlement of the dowry. The dowry, which is given by the bride's family, provides the bride with money for possible hard times ahead. It is not the price given to the groom for marrying her.

The Islamic bride is treated to full-body treatments in which all bodily hair is waxed off and her skin is rubbed with herbs. Her hands and feet are intricately decorated with henna.

A traditional week-long or modern two-day celebration is launched with a motorcade of honking, decorated cars. The bride and groom are royally dressed and seated on a dais for family and friends to admire. Men and women go to separate areas to enjoy the wedding dinner.

After everyone has eaten, the bride walks around her father's house seven times to bid farewell before going to start a new life with her husband. Meanwhile the groom is taken out to the town by friends and then left at his door before bedtime.

DEATH Wherever possible, a Muslim funeral takes place on the same day as the death. Female relatives and friends cleanse and dress the body for burial. Male mourners and friends carry the body on a bier to the cemetery, led by a man reading the Qur'an. Islamic headstones are very simple structures.

LABOR

The working conditions of workers are safeguarded by the 1966 Labor Code: This includes minimum wage rates for the different occupations, a six-day workweek for agricultural workers, and a five-day week of forty to forty-eight hours for all other workers. The code stipulates an annual paid vacation of up to eighteen working days, and maternity leave of four to six weeks.

The Agricultural Labor Code grants severance pay, wage increments, and bonuses to farmworkers based on harvest size, skill, and seniority. One-third of the labor force works in the agricultural sector, and these benefits reward workers for greater production while also taking care of their needs.

THE IMPORTANCE OF KINSHIP Generally speaking, Tunisians prefer not to work in hierarchical and authoritarian settings. They believe that paid employment for its own sake is undignified. Self-respect, independence, and pride are greatly prized. Materialism is not a traditional Tunisian characteristic, and good interpersonal ties are more effective than money and status in motivating Tunisian workers to excel.

The Tunisian management style is to show concern for workers, build teamwork, and make everyone equally responsible for productivity. Workers are encouraged to help one another. Differences in status are blurred, and learning is promoted.

Kinship ties—determined by people from the same family, region, village, or school—bring immediate loyalty. Blood and clan ties are always more important than mere friendship. This tradition goes back to the days when a clan lived in a village together and looked out for its members.

BUSINESS ETIQUETTE In general, Tunisians follow the business etiquette of the French. Upon meeting, people shake hands and exchange business cards that are usually written in French, which is the language of commerce in Tunisia. Meetings over lunch and dinner or even on weekends are acceptable. Many Tunisian men are not attuned to the relatively new idea of equality, and do not bring their wives to business functions. They usually do not discuss their families or personal affairs with business associates.

BUSINESS HOURS Business hours in cities depend on the place of work. Government and public sector offices are open all day, Mondays through Thursdays, except for a two-hour midday break, and half a day on Fridays and Saturdays. Banks are open Mondays to Fridays except for a two-hour midday break. In summer offices open very early, many at 7:30 a.m., and close in the early afternoon, at about 1:30 p.m. This allows people to enjoy the longer summer daylight hours and avoid working in the oppressive afternoon heat.

Shopkeepers and taxi drivers also observe a two-hour midday break. During the month of Ramadan (a variable month, following an Islamic calendar), when Muslims fast from sunrise to sunset, shopkeepers close promptly at sunset to observe the daily prayer and the breaking of the fast. Many, however, reopen their shops in the evening, as Muslims stock up for the festival that is held at the end of Ramadan.

INTERNET LINKS

https://www.awid.org/news-and-analysis/marriage-and-divorce-tunisia-womens-rights
This site addresses women's rights in Tunisia.

https://www.unicef.org/infobycountry/Tunisia_statistics.html
UNICEF provides a range of statistics about Tunisian life on this page.

RELIGION

The Great Mosque of Zaytuna in the Medina of Tunis dates to 863 CE.

8

TUNISIAN SOCIETY IS MORE THAN 99 percent Muslim, and Islam is more than a religion. It's a way of living—one which pervades all aspects of social, cultural, and ethical life. Despite the overwhelming majority status of Islam, Tunisians respect religious freedom. Most Tunisians are Sunni Muslims, but there are small groups of Kharijites and the mystical Sufis. Christians, mostly French and Italian Roman Catholics, and Jews together make up less than 1 percent of the population.

In Arab culture there is the strong belief that envious, and even admiring, glances bring bad luck, or the "evil eye." Tunisians ward off the evil eye by reciting aloud certain formulas and incantations.

ISLAM

The founder of Islam, Muhammad ibn Abdallah (570–632 CE), was orphaned and brought up by relatives in Mecca, in today's Saudi Arabia. At that time, Mecca was a center of pagan life, where tradesmen made profits from visitors to the pagan shrines. In 610 CE, Muhammad began to receive revelations from Allah (God) through the angel Gabriel, who taught Muhammad to recite the word of God. He wrote down the revelations, which make up part of the Qur'an, the Islamic holy book. Muslims refer to Muhammad as the Prophet, the last in a line of prophets, including Jesus Christ before him, who are written about in the Bible.

Muhammad denounced the idol worship of his time, which, in turn, alienated the powerful merchants. To avoid assassination, Muhammad fled to Yathrib (modern-day Medina, in Saudi Arabia) in June 622. There, Muhammad was invited to be the ruler. He set up a theocratic state with moral and legal codes for his people, then fought the Meccans and defeated them. Islam spread rapidly from then on, as followers traveled far and wide and conquered lands to spread the religion. By 630, two years before Muhammad's death, Islam had spread through all of Arabia. By 670 it had reached Kairouan in Tunisia through Uqba ibn Nafi.

ISLAMIC SECTS

After Muhammad died, and his followers tried to choose his successor, or caliph (from the word *khalifah*, Arabic for "successor"), there was a deep disagreement which led to the rise of the two main Islamic factions—the Sunni and the Shia. The Sunnis believed that caliphs should be elected, and so they supported the first caliph, Abu Bakar, the Prophet Muhammad's father-in-law. The Shias, on the other hand, believed that only the Prophet Muhammad's direct descendants should rule, and so they supported Ali, the fourth caliph, the Prophet Muhammad's cousin and son-in-law. Sunnis, who make up the largest sect worldwide, follow the teaching in the Hadith (the Islamic oral law).

Radical sects have also risen over the centuries. Among them are Fatimids (a Shia group claiming descent from Fatima, the Prophet Muhammad's daughter), Kharijites (a liberal sect, popular among poor Berbers, that promotes the idea that any Muslim could be caliph), and the Sufis.

SUNNI ISLAM The Sunnis recognize four schools of Islamic law—the Malikite school that is popular in North and sub-Saharan Africa; the Hanifite school in Turkey, India, and China; the Ibadi school in Saudi Arabia; and the Shafiite school in Egypt, India, and Southeast Asia. These schools differ in the details of the practice of Islam, but they do not question its dogma. They came into existence in the second century of the Islamic era (the ninth

ISLAMIC TEXTS

The word Qur'an *means "recitation," because, in reciting it, a Muslim feels the poetry of God's word. Muhammad was taught to recite the word of God, and he, in turn, taught his followers. Since many people were illiterate during Muhammad's time, recitation was the best way to spread the new religion. These recitations were collected and written down, eighteen years after Muhammad's death, in 650 CE. They are divided into 114 chapters, or* sura, *arranged from the longest to the shortest. Each sura is named. There are four parts in the Qur'an: worship of Allah, the day of judgment, proclamations and stories of earlier prophets, and social laws. A set of commands encourages charity, kindness, sobriety, and humility, and prohibits murder, adultery, idolatry, and meanness. No one is allowed to alter the Qur'an.*

The Hadith, also known as the Sunna, comprises the collected sayings, teachings, and characteristics of the Prophet Muhammad's personal behavior, recorded by those who knew him. Following the example of the Prophet Muhammad's life is a prerequisite to being a good Muslim. The Hadith is not an alternative to the Qur'an. Sunni Muslims recognize the Hadith as a basis of Muslim law, but Shia Muslims do not.

Interpretations from the Qur'an and Hadith form the shariah, a legal system that guides the spiritual, ethical, and social life of Muslims. In traditional Islamic countries, civil, criminal, and spiritual sins are judged according to shariah laws. Shariah courts were abolished in Tunisia in 1957, but Islamic fundamentalists are fighting to have them reinstated.

century), when Muslim thinkers met to lay down shariah laws. Most Tunisian Muslims adhere to the Malikite school.

SUFISM This mystical sect originated in Persia in the ninth century CE. *Suf* is Arabic for "wool," and the first Sufi believers wore woolen robes. Sufis are not satisfied simply to follow Islamic law. To bring them closer to God, they perform rituals that include recitation, music, and dance. Many Sufis are ascetics who renounce materialism, believing that this brings them to a higher state of virtue. Their religious centers, or *zaouia* (zo-EE-ya), are found mainly in the region of Nefta, north of Chott el Djerid. Sufis believe that their masters, Shaykh, possess *baraka* (BAH-ra-kah; "blessedness" or "spiritual powers") and are *marabouts* (saints). Shrines are built above their graves, and their powers are believed to transfer to those who visit the graves.

KHARIJITES The Kharijite movement arose in Morocco to oppose Arab leadership of Islam—in particular, the selection of the caliph based on race, station, or descent from the Prophet Muhammad. The Kharijites proposed that any Muslim could be the religious leader. This idea appealed to the Berbers in Ifriqiya, who resented the elite Arabs. Berber Kharijites invaded Kairouan during the rule of the Umayyads. They set up tribal kingdoms and fought the Abbasids (who followed the Umayyads).

The Kharijites continued to exist in great numbers until the tenth century, when the Fatimids, another Islamic group, took control of Ifriqiya and began to persecute them. The Kharijites took refuge on Djerba Island, where they live to this day. They are known for their austerity and the more than three hundred mosques on the island, which are simply designed.

FOLK BELIEFS AND SUPERSTITIONS

Folk beliefs have merged with Islam from the very early days of the religion. Many Muslims in Tunisia, for example, believe in the existence of *baraka*, or spiritual powers, in some individuals, and that these are transferable to others. They believe that the Prophet Muhammad had the most powerful baraka, and that others who possess it are marabouts. Proof of the possession of baraka is seen in the performance of miracles, amazing spiritual insight, or a bloodline connection to someone who possessed it earlier.

In the past, marabouts were influential throughout the countryside as mediators in family and tribal disputes. Today they have a role only in remote areas of central and southern Tunisia. These holy men built centers where they taught, slept, and were buried. They had followers or brotherhoods through whom Islam spread rapidly in Tunisia. Sufism very likely developed out of some of these ideas.

In the remote parts of Tunisia, superstitions stemming from ancient practices have blended with the practice of Islam. The idea of evil spirits called *djinns*, which often take the form of animals, is common. To protect themselves from djinns, some people wear amulets inscribed with Qur'anic verses; others toss bits of meat into dark corners to placate the djinns. Certain stones are believed to possess magical properties; the bloodstone, for example, is believed to protect against toothache. With the spread of modern education, superstitious religious beliefs are dying out in Tunisia.

A shrine for marabout sits atop a cliff overlooking the city of Ghomrassen.

JUDAISM

The history of the Jews is told in the Old Testament of the Bible. The Jews believe that they are the "children of Abraham" (one of the founders of Judaism) and God's chosen people. Jewish sacred texts include the Torah (the first five books of the Bible, attributed to the Prophet Moses and written on parchment scrolls) and the Talmud (law and tradition).

Jews have lived in Tunisia since ancient times. A small Jewish community of approximately one thousand people, consisting of mainly merchants or skilled craftspeople, remains on Djerba Island. The most famous synagogue in Tunisia is the El Ghriba ("Marvelous") Synagogue on Djerba Island, one of the holiest Jewish places in North Africa. Jewish pilgrims from all around the world visit it. A sacred cavern inside the synagogue contains one of the oldest Torahs in the world.

CHRISTIANITY

Christianity was the dominant religion in Tunisia during the Roman and Byzantine periods of rule. In 170 CE, a Latin church was built in Carthage, and the holy scriptures were taught in Latin. Until the arrival of the Arabs, Tunisia

THE FIVE PILLARS OF ISLAM

The five pillars of Islam are the five practices/duties incumbent on every Muslim. They are: Shahadah—professing faith ("There is no god but God, and Muhammad is his prophet"); Salah—praying five times daily; Zakah—giving alms (fixed at 1/40th of personal income but voluntary today); Sawm—fasting during Ramadan; and Hajj—making a pilgrimage to Mecca.

Muslims wash themselves in a prescribed way with water or sand before praying at dawn, midday, midafternoon, sunset, and nightfall. Facing the direction of Mecca, the worshipper adopts three positions—standing, bowing, and prostrating—symbolizing the superiority of reason over instinct, being a servant before a master, and submitting to the will of God. Whenever possible, men gather to pray in a mosque under the leadership of an imam (prayer leader); on Fridays they are obliged to do so at noon.

Prayer in a mosque is followed by a khutba *(sermon). Women who attend public worship are segregated from the men. Most women prefer to pray in the privacy of their homes.*

Fasting throughout Ramadan, the ninth month of the Islamic calendar, is compulsory for all Muslims except the sick, very young children, nursing mothers, pregnant women, the old, and travelers. Fasting means abstinence from eating, drinking, and other indulgences from dawn to sunset.

Every Muslim should make the pilgrimage to Mecca at least once. During the hajj, Muslims dress in a white, seamless garment (called an ihraam*) and abstain from shaving, cutting their hair or nails. Rites performed during the hajj include kissing the sacred black stone (the Muslim object of veneration, built into the eastern wall of the Ka'abah—a small shrine within the Great Mosque of Mecca, and probably dating from the pre-Islamic religion of the Arabs), going around the Ka'abah, running seven times between the hills of Safa and Marwa, and standing in prayer at the Plain of Arafat.*

was a major cultural and religious center for the Christian West. In 256 CE, about eighty bishops met at a council in Carthage.

Christianity was never a religion of the poor masses in Tunisia. It was popular mainly among the educated and rich—the ruling class, or property owners. Then a group called the Donatists began to espouse the cause of the poor. The Donatists came into existence in Tunisia when a conflict arose over the ordination of a bishop named Caecilian in Carthage in 312 CE. (The Donatists supported Caecilian's rival, Donatus.) They were a dominant Christian group in the fourth century, known particularly for their martyrdom during the period of their persecution from 317 to 321 CE. The group faded away gradually after a conference in Carthage in 411 CE denied the Donatists civil and ecclesiastical rights.

INTERNET LINKS

https://www.loc.gov/law/help/tunisia.php
The Law Library of the Library of Congress reports on the role of Islamic law in Tunisia's new constitution.

https://www.state.gov/documents/organization/193121.pdf
This report from the US Department of State assesses religious freedom in Tunisia.

https://www.wsj.com/articles/insular-jewish-community-of-djerba-tunisia-has-weathered-revolution-and-terrorism-but-can-it-survive-girls-education-1423869146
This in-depth article explores the community of Tunisian Jews on Djerba Island.

LANGUAGE

A road sign is written in Arabic and French.

A RABIC IS THE LANGUAGE OF Northern Africa, and throughout the Maghreb. Universally spoken and understood, it is Tunisia's official language. Some two-thirds of the Tunisian population also speak French, which is considered the language of commerce—it is widely used in government and business, and is important socially. The French language gives its speakers a mark of sophistication and education. Although the bilingual, educated elite correspond in French, advertisements directed at the average Tunisian are written in Arabic. The Berber language, Tamazight, is spoken by less than 1 percent of the population.

ARABIC

Four varieties of Arabic are used in Tunisia: classical, modern literary (or modern standard), colloquial (dialect), and intermediary (or "educated"). Classical Arabic is the language of the Qur'an and represents the ideal

in primary schools, children are taught in Arabic. In the third year, French is introduced as a second language. Secondary school students have a bilingual option; arts and social science subjects are taught in Arabic, while the sciences are taught in French. At the University of Tunis, French is the language of instruction in all subjects except for theology, law, and Arabic literature and language.

that Muslims strive to achieve. As the vehicle of historical, literary, and religious heritage, it is used mainly for religious purposes.

Modern literary Arabic is a simplification of classical Arabic. In Tunisia it is the official language of the media, government documents, literature, and education. For most Tunisian adults, however, it is a language that can only be understood after formal study. The government has been promoting modern literary Arabic through lessons over television and radio, but without much success.

Most Tunisians prefer to use intermediary Arabic. It is a mixture of colloquial and modern literary Arabic and is increasingly being used by the media, government, and intellectuals to communicate with the general population.

Variations of Arabic dialect occur in Tunisia, but they are generally understood by everyone. Franco-Arabic, a blending of Arabic with specialized French terms and turns of speech, is an urban dialect spoken by students, government officials, and professionals. The urban and coastal dialects are closer to classical Arabic and similar to other dialects found in North African cities. In the interior, the Arabic dialect is heavily peppered with Berber words and has low prestige.

THE POLITICS OF LANGUAGE

The issue of language has been given great attention in the Maghreb. Newly independent countries were determined to erase colonial influence by replacing the dominant European language with Arabic. Arabization, or the spread of Arab culture through language, has been more passionately promoted in other Maghreb countries than it has in Tunisia, where the policy has been a gradual spread of Arabic, while retaining the popular use of French. In the early years of self-government, the French-educated president Habib Bourguiba (in office 1957—1987) promoted French to such an extent that it caused resentment among the people. He subsequently moderated his policies.

Arabization has not been smooth in Tunisia. Modern literary Arabic was first chosen as the language of government and media, but most Tunisians did not understand it, since only a minority spoke it. The government adopted a pragmatic approach and conceded that the friendlier intermediary Arabic was more useful. To be employed in the government services, proficiency in modern literary Arabic is required, although French is used in internal communications. In medicine, technology, and science, French is essential.

THE MEDIA

There are state-owned and private broadcast networks, and a large number of newspapers and magazines published and distributed in Tunisia, in both Arabic and French. In 2015, about 48.5 percent of Tunisians used the Internet.

Prior to the Arab Spring, media censorship in Tunisia under longtime dictator Zine El Abidine Ben Ali was extremely strict. Criticism of government officials or state institutions caused many publications to be seized or suspended. Since the 2011 revolution, however, Tunisia has enjoyed unprecedented freedom of expression. In fact, the country ranked first in North Africa in the 2017 World Press Freedom Index published by Reporters Without Borders (RSF). However, that same year, the organization, along with other non-governmental watchdog groups, including the Tunisian Press Syndicate and Amnesty International, warned that freedom of the press appeared to be deteriorating in Tunisia. In 2017, the US-based Freedom House human rights organization determined Tunisia's freedom of the press as "partly free."

INTERNET LINKS

https://freedomhouse.org/report/freedom-world/2017/tunisia
This is the 2017 Freedom House profile of Tunisia. More recent years will be available on this same site.

http://www.omniglot.com/writing/arabic.htm
This is an introduction to Arabic. Omniglot also offers overviews of the various types of Arabic language.

ARTS

A vendor shows off a traditional brass plate at a marketplace in the medina section of Tunis.

U NDER THE DICTATORSHIP OF President Zine El Abidine Ben Ali, as is typical under oppressive governments, artistic expression was suppressed. Many Tunisian artists had to look overseas for a safer, more open environment in which to market their work. The government closed down some arts and music institutions in order to quell dissent. Since the 2011 revolution, however, the contemporary arts scene in the country has emerged with more vitality.

Nevertheless, artistic freedom still faces challenges from the conservative Muslim community, which opposes a wide spectrum of artistic expression as blasphemous and immoral. Meanwhile, ancient crafts such as carpet weaving and pottery remain important and widely accepted artistic activities.

ARCHITECTURE

PHOENICIAN Excavations at Cape Bon of Carthaginian houses on Byrsa Hill, and a fifth-century BCE walled town in Kerkouane reveal that the Phoenicians might have based their models on Greek buildings. Tiled floors had inset pieces of marble, and walls were covered in stucco and

10

Tunisia was, for many years, a popular location for desert movie sets. Famous movies filmed in the country include *Star Wars* (1977), *Monty Python's Life of Brian* (1979), *Raiders of the Lost Ark* (1981), *The English Patient* (1996), *Star Wars: Episode I: The Phantom Menace* (1999), and *Star Wars: Episode II—Attack of the Clones* (2002).

Egyptian Pharaonic art. Punic temples also seem to be copied from the Greeks and Egyptians. The third-century Dougga Punic mausoleum, a pointed tower monument, is still intact.

ROMAN The hallmarks of Roman architecture can be seen in the Carthage aqueduct; El Jem amphitheater; theaters at Médenine, Chemtou, and Bulla Regia; and triumphal arches throughout Tunisia. The Romans developed cement and concrete and discovered how to build the arch and vault so that pillars were not needed to support the roof of a building. Only in the design of temples did they use the indigenous tradition of worshipping in an outdoor enclosure, as at the sanctuary of Saturn at Dougga. Some temples built by the Romans were dedicated to Moorish gods, but more often they were built for Roman gods that were modifications of Phoenician gods. The god Baal Hammon, for example, became the Roman god Saturn, who had a strong cult following in the countryside until the fifth century.

The ancient Roman amphitheater of El Jem once held 35,000 spectators. Today it is a **UNESCO World Heritage Site.**

BYZANTIUM CHRISTIAN Byzantine architecture, seen in churches or basilicas, was inspired by the design of Roman public buildings. Church ruins at many sites (a famous one is Sbeïtla) come with naves, mosaic art, tombstones, altars, pillars, and baptisteries. The many fortresses built around forums, temples, and baths have helped preserve Roman sites. The most impressive ones can be seen at Haïdra, Ksar Lemsa, Mustim, Bordj Brahim, and Aïn Tounga.

ISLAMIC ARCHITECTURE The grandeur of Islamic architecture in Tunisia is seen in the mosques, shrines, public buildings, and homes of the wealthy, which are embellished with domes, minarets, and arches. The oldest Islamic buildings are *ribats* (ri-BAHTs), or fortified monasteries.

The basic design of a mosque is a simple open courtyard, enclosed by a high windowless wall, which contains a fountain or wash area for the ritual cleansing before prayer. At the end of the courtyard is a roofed and carpeted

Traditional Arabic architecture is richly decorated with mosaics.

prayer hall. Inside there is a mihrab, a niche indicating the direction of Mecca. In large mosques there is also a *minbar*, or pulpit, where the prayer leader (imam) conducts special prayers on Friday. A minaret towers over the building. The basic plan of the mosque has been modified over the centuries to include lodgings for visitors or students, and classrooms for Qur'anic schools.

The first Tunisian mosques followed Byzantine church models, including their domes, arches, and high bell towers, which the Muslims used as minarets. The great mosques of Kairouan and Tunis are examples of Byzantine influence. There the prayer halls are supported by rows of horseshoe-shaped arches resting on pillars salvaged from Roman buildings. Huge domes top the buildings.

Later there was a movement away from using highly decorated columns and capitals and toward the use of clean pillars and arches. The new design focused on proportion, simplicity of form, elegant stonework, and calligraphic friezes. The great mosques of Sousse, Sfax, and Mahdia are examples of classical simplicity.

In the eleventh century Moorish architecture was introduced under the Almohad and Hafsid caliphs. Most of the architecture of this period has been destroyed, but the Kasbah Mosque in Tunis is an excellent example of Moorish architecture. Under the seventeenth-century beys, Ottoman Turkish styles were imported: octagonal minarets, marble inlay, Andalusian (Spanish Muslim) tiles, Moorish carved plaster, and painted woodwork. In the flurry of decoration, proportion and simplicity were lost. The Husseinids favored external windows and decoration. The Tourbet el Bey, Mosque des Teinturiers, and the Sahib et Tabaa Mosque are a few examples.

TOWNS AND FORTIFIED BUILDINGS With the arrival of the Arabs in the seventh century, architectural design was influenced by the need for defensive features. A holy war was being fought. Early towns and villages were built with high surrounding walls with towers and thick gates, or *bab* (BEHB).

Among the forts and citadels scattered throughout Tunisia is the Kef Kasbar on the top of a hill. Monasteries (*ribats*), resting places for travelers (*fondouk*), and even buildings to store food were built defensively, some of

them (the *ghorfa* [GHOR-fa], for example) by Berbers as defense against the Arabs.

Sidi Bou Said in northern Tunisia is known for the use of blue and white in its architecture.

HOMES AND PUBLIC BUILDINGS The plan of the North African house has been the same for many centuries. Rooms for eating, cooking, and sleeping are built around a courtyard used by the women of the house. The courtyard often has a well or cistern for water and is a private space screened from public view by a hall, zigzag passage, or screen. In the old days the courtyard had an arcade, while the rooms had plaster walls tiled in the lower half and painted wooden ceilings. Today whitewashed concrete is the pragmatic choice.

COLONIAL ERA During the nineteenth and twentieth century years under French rule, many new buildings were constructed in Tunis reflecting the European standards of the day. Architects combined the European neo-classical design with influences of North African aesthetics to create a style that came to be called arabiscance. Many of those colonial era buildings are in disrepair today.

The Bardo Museum in Tunis is one of the largest and most important museums in North Africa. Its collections include archaeological treasures from numerous civilizations over thousands of years of Tunisian history.

The museum is part of a building complex in Tunis that also includes the National Assembly and an old arsenal. The museum building itself, originally a fifteenth-century Hafsid dynasty palace, is architecturally impressive, with Islamic-style porticos, cupolas, galleries, and vaulted ceilings that date from the Ottoman period.

Many of the Bardo's collections are named after the location of the excavations; for example, there are Mahdia, Sousse, and Carthage rooms. Bardo Museum is known especially for its Carthaginian collection and its rich Roman and Byzantine mosaics. The only known portrait of the Latin poet Virgil is found there, in a mosaic measuring 1,475 square feet (137 square m). This is believed to be the largest mosaic portrait in existence.

The collection devoted to Tunisia's early history features the Hermaion monument from the Middle Paleolithic era (ca. 40,000 BCE). This monument—a pyramid of stone balls, carved flints, and animal bones—was dedicated to the spirit of a stream.

The Roman and pre-Christian exhibits include ornamental tiling from the first church in Tunisia, dating to the fourth century CE; statues of the ancient Greek and Roman gods Apollo, Asclepius, and Ceres; a third-century mosaic of the Greek god Dionysus giving a vine to a peasant; and Roman funerary glassware, pottery, and statuettes.

The Islamic collection contains beautiful books of calligraphy, including the extraordinary Blue Qur'an of Kairouan, which is embellished with gold writing.

MOSAICS

The Bardo Museum in Tunis has a rich collection of Roman mosaics dating from the second to the sixth centuries CE. The earliest known mosaic, discovered in Carthage, dates from the fifth or fourth century BCE. The Phoenicians first used this art form, and the Romans popularized it.

Roman mosaics of the early first century BCE were simple and flat. Later they became more sophisticated and included geometric patterns. Some early African mosaics included polychrome panels in the borders, imported ready-made from Italy. Italian craftsmen brought over during this period to train people eventually set up their own workshops. Those at El Djem and Sousse were so successful that their mosaics decorated public buildings. Each workshop was known for its distinctive style.

By the second century CE, mosaics were being produced in richer colors and with more complex compositions. The themes of mosaic art include the seasons, banquets, hunting, mythology, and gladiators. At Bulla Regia, an archaeological site in northwestern Tunisia, there is a mosaic of Venus being carried by centaurs in a cockleshell flanked by two dolphins. In El Djem, mosaics decorated the Trajan Baths of 115 to 120 CE with a depiction of Dionysus with satyrs, nymphs, and centaurs; the Thiasos Baths have a large marine scene. From the mid-third century CE production declined and the form became more impressionistic and less detailed.

The golden age of mosaics was in the fourth and fifth centuries, when an abstract style evolved, with vivid stripes replacing subtle gradations of color. In the Christian era of the late fourth century, mosaics were used to decorate churches. These often large and floral compositions were mainly geometric and included popular images such as scrolling vines, the Christian symbols of fishes, and the Greek letters alpha and omega. Tomb mosaics, a form unique to Africa, also date to the Christian era. Often they had inscriptions, were nonfigurative (one example, in Kelibia, has ornamental borders and an epitaph in a crown flanked by a pair of palm trees), and sometimes had half- or full-length portraits of the deceased, such as those in Sfax and Tabarka.

CRAFTS

CARPETS, KLIMS, AND MERGOUMS Carpets are made of separate hand-knotted strands, while klims (or kilims) and mergoums are tapestry ground covers woven as a single layer. Carpet-making is regulated by a government-controlled agency that standardizes patterns and tags a carpet by the number of knots per square meter. Many Tunisian carpets have a white or light background with blue and red patterns similar to Berber and Persian designs. Large carpets take several years to make and can last several lifetimes.

Klims have geometric patterns with lines broken by diamonds, lozenges, and zigzags. In mergoums, designs are emphasized by over-stitching and embellishing done with tassels and sequins. Themes include human and animal figures, Islamic legends, designs from Roman mosaics, and desert landscapes.

CERAMICS Tunisian pottery consists of figurines, jugs, and wall tiles. The Andalusian style most common today includes yellow, blue, and green patterns separated by bands of thick black lines, as well as by geometric designs. One of the most popular kinds is a shiny tile with metallic glints.

METALWORK, LEATHERCRAFT, AND WOODWORK Engraved brass and copper vases, ashtrays, plates, intricate wrought-iron window grills, and blue and white birdcages are popular in Tunisia.

Like other crafts, leather goods—including sturdy and fashionable belts, saddles, and handbags—can be found all over Tunisia, especially in the souks. Olive wood carved into bowls, spoons, chessboards, boxes, and sculptures are expertly made. Sfax, the olive oil capital, has the best selection.

CALLIGRAPHY AND IMAGERY

Texts from the Qur'an are often the inspiration for Islamic art. Caliph Abdel Malik (685—705 CE) identified two schools of Arabic script: *kufic* and cursive. *Kufic* is an angular, solid, hieratic script, suitable for carved and ornamental texts. Cursive is rounder and more flowing. Calligraphy is frequently used to decorate sacred books and the walls of religious buildings, and is carved in stone and wood and painted on ceramic tiles.

The development of calligraphy can be seen in the early copies of the Qur'an. The oldest, dating from the eighth century, is written in a pronounced cursive style. *Kufic*, with interlacing stylized plant motifs, became the preferred religious script in the ninth century. The Bardo Museum has the famous ninth- and tenth-century Blue Qur'an, in which verses are written in golden letters on blue parchment.

A leaf from the famous Blue Qur'an shows the gold script on deep blue parchment.

Images of fish and Fatima's hand are used in jewelry designs, because they are believed to bring the bearer good luck. Fish symbolize fertility and the *Hamsa*, or "hand of Fatima" symbol is said to ward off evil. This stylized palm, with fingers outstretched, often with an eye in the palm, is worn as an amulet by Muslim women.

FILM

In the late 1960s, the Fédération Panafricaine des Cinéastes, a pan-African cinema federation, was formed. Being well established by then, Tunisian cinema developed a variety of genres, ranging from comedy, political, and poetic to sociological and psychological. In 1994 Tunisian women entered the world of film directors when Moufida Tlatli's first feature film, *The Silence of the Palace*, won a prize at the Cannes Film Festival. More recently, the Tunisian moviemakers Ferid Boughedir, Nouri Bouzid, Wassim Béji, and Abdellatif Kechiche have been honored for their contributions to North African cinema.

Since the 2011 revolution, new Tunisian documentary films have addressed political and cultural issues that would have been impossible to present just a few years ago. Tunisian director Mohamed Zran's film *Degage* is about the revolution itself, while the 2012 film *Babylon,* directed by Youssef Chebbi and Ala Eddine Slim, focuses on a Libyan refugee camp in Tunisia. *The Black Memory* by director Hichem Ben Ammar examines the imprisonment and torture of leftist activists during the regime of President Habib Bourguiba.

Despite this newfound freedom, certain films remain off-limits in Tunisia because their subject matter is deemed culturally and religiously too offensive. Tunisian-French director Abdellatif Kechiche's film *Blue is the Warmest Color* (2013), which won the top award at the 2013 Cannes Film Festival, may never be seen in Tunisia itself because it deals very openly with homosexuality.

LITERATURE

Arabic is the main language of modern Tunisian literature, followed by French, which is used in novellas and plays. In the past, centers of Arabic literature included Kairouan, Mahdia, and Tunis. Subjects included praise for the rulers and theology. In the later years of Arab Tunisia, the focus shifted to Tunisia's African identity.

One of the best-known Tunisian writers is Albert Memmi (b. 1920), a Tunisian Jew living in Paris. He writes in French and his works are regularly translated into English. Another well-known Tunisian writer living abroad is Mustapha Tlili (b. 1937), who lives in the United States and writes novels in French. His novel, *Lion Mountain* (1988), dealing with Tunisian corruption, was banned in Tunisia. Popular Tunisian writers include Walid Soliman (b. 1975) and the prolific novelist and poet Hédi André Bouraoui (b. 1932), who lives in Canada.

There are very few works of literature written in Tunisian Arabic. In the past, a large body of folktales and poems were handed down orally by wandering storytellers at marketplaces and festivals. Most modern Tunisian authors like to write in standard Arabic or in French. Sometimes the dialogue in a novel will be in Tunisian Arabic, but the main narrative will be in standard Arabic. Folk lyrics for popular local songs are also usually written in Tunisian Arabic.

MUSIC

The most typical traditional Tunisian style of music is *malouf*, which means "familiar" or "customary." This music, which is based on a kind of classical Arab poetry, is popular across Northern Africa, with each country having its own somewhat different versions. Originating from Andalusia in southern Spain, malouf is played by a five-piece band with a violin, flute, zither, lute, and underarm drum.

INTERNET LINKS

http://www.bardomuseum.tn
This site of the Bardo Museum in Tunis offers an English language option.

http://www.discovertunisia.com/en/tunisie-arts-and-crafts/regional-crafts
This site shows examples of some of Tunisia's traditional arts and crafts.

http://www.getty.edu/conservation/our_projects/education/bulla/overview.html
This conservation site offers a slide show of mosaics and other ruins at the Bulla Regia site.

https://www.theguardian.com/film/2015/dec/03/star-wars-abandoned-tunisian-locations-in-pictures
The abandoned Star Wars film sets in Tunisia, with numerous photos, are the subject of this article.

http://www.tourismtunisia.com/tunisian-mosaics
This tourism site offers several good examples of ancient Tunisian mosaics.

http://www.tunisia-live.net/2014/05/07/hidden-gems-of-tunis-colonial-era-architecture
This article includes numerous photos of colonial era architecture in Tunis.

LEISURE

A boy plays soccer in a park in Tunis.

11

O RDINARY TUNISIANS GENERALLY spend their leisure time relaxing with friends and family. Men like to gather at cafés and play dominoes, checkers, or cards; talk about soccer, and smoke *chichas* (hookahs). These get-togethers are strictly male-only—any mixed crowds at a Tunisian café are most likely tourists. Tunisian women, likewise, find companionship with other women, while shopping or at home.

SOCCER

Soccer, or football, is the country's favorite sport. Tunisia has its own national, city, and village soccer teams, and the country has competed in international tournaments such as the World Cup and the Mediterranean, Maghreb, Arab, and African leagues. Soccer is so infused in the country's cultural identity that some hotels have regular matches organized between staff and guests.

The national team is called the Eagles of Carthage. In 2004, Tunisia hosted and eventually won the African Cup of Nations soccer tournament, making the nation the soccer champion of the continent for the first time. Despite the fact that Tunisia has a good soccer league, the best Tunisian soccer players often move to Europe to play in the major leagues in France, Spain, Italy, and England.

Tunisian soccer star Tarak Dhiab (b. 1954) was named the African Footballer of the Year in 1977 and Best Tunisian Player of the Century by the Confederation of African Football (CAF). He went on to have a career as a soccer analyst for Al Jazeera Sports, and in 2011, became Tunisia's Minister of Youth and Sports under Prime Minister Hamadi Jebali.

Kayaks sit in a beach at a typical beach resort on the Tunisian coast.

WATER SPORTS

Blessed with roughly 700 miles (1,127 km) of coastland, gentle Mediterranean weather, and warm clear waters, Tunisia's abundant beaches in the north and along the eastern coast offer a plethora of activities on sand and surf. From rocky to sandy beaches, populous resorts to isolated beaches, Tunisians and tourists have plenty of choices.

Tunisia enjoys a longer sailing season than northern Mediterranean countries do, and conditions for sailing are good all along the coast. There are yachting marinas at Port El Kantaoui, Monastir, Sidi Bou Saïd, and Tabarka. They also have resorts, hotels, restaurants, banks, shops, and other conveniences.

Snorkeling and scuba diving are popular activities, especially at Tabarka, an ancient coral trading center. There are diving centers for amateurs equipped with boats, professional instructors, diving monitors, and specialized gear in Monastir and the new seaside resorts in Tabarka, Port El Kantaoui, and Sousse.

Locals and tourists have a choice of swimming in either the ocean or in countless hotel pools. Hotels often also rent equipment and offer instructors for water polo, waterskiing, windsurfing, and parasailing.

Regular fishers frequent the fishing and trading ports and have lots of advice to offer and stories to tell about their fishing adventures. Besides fish and shellfish, one can find octopi off the Kerkenna Islands, and coral on the Tabarka coast. Tuna fishing is especially good at Sidi Daoud on Cape Bon.

SPAS

Tunisian culture has a long tradition of public bathing, which dates to Roman times. Today, bathing is largely a therapeutic activity for those who can afford it.

THALASSOTHERAPY CENTERS These "sea water care" centers are like ocean spas with seawater pools and therapists who use specialized fitness equipment. This type of therapy, based on the healing powers of sea water, began in France in the late nineteenth century and is said to help with back problems, joints, and muscle pain, as well as with skin conditions. It's also simply very relaxing. There are underwater massage baths, Jacuzzis, power and spray showers, bubbling gymnastic pools, massage booths, and mud and algae treatments. A whole range of treatments is offered, including beauty therapy, fitness and anti-stress treatment, algae therapy, bio-marine therapy and relaxation, postnatal therapy, and diet. The first one was built in Sousse at the Abou Nawas Boujaafar Hotel.

A patron enjoys the thalassotherapy spa at a seaside resort in Hammamet.

THERMAL SPRINGS Traditionally healing waters draw the ailing and stressed. Three locations in Tunisia have been developed into healing centers: Hammam Bourguiba, between Tabarka and Ain Draham, has springs with waters prescribed for inflammation, infection, or allergic upper respiratory complaints; Korbous on Cape Bon has waters that are supposed to cure chronic rheumatism, arthritis, and afflictions of the nervous system; and Djebel Oust in Zaghouan has waters that treat rheumatism and other arthritic diseases.

HUNTING

Wild boar and game-bird hunting have been popular traditional sports in Tunisia for centuries. The wild boar season runs from mid-October to the end of January, and hunting takes place in the dunes, hills, and mountains of the Kroumirie region.

The traditional hunting technique used is *battue* (the French word for "round up" or "beat"). It involves beating the bush to flush out wild boar. Firecrackers and dogs are used as well.

OTHER SPORTS

GOLF Golf is an increasingly popular sport, and several major courses have recently been built in Tabarka, Hammamet, and Port El Kantaoui. The Port El Kantaoui golf course is of international quality, with twenty-seven holes and three obstacle-filled courses.

SAND YACHTING This activity is practiced on the dunes near Kébili and Douz. A sand yacht is a three-wheeled boat with a sail, rudder, seat, and pedals.

HIKING Tunisia has hiking trails in the mountainous north among the cork oak—covered Kroumirie Mountains and on the gentle slopes of Zaghouan, Kasserine, Ain Durham, and El Kef. For those who prefer a different landscape, hiking trips across the desert south are also available. Walking four or five days across the Grand Eastern Erg is an experience for the fit and adventurous.

HORSEBACK RIDING AND RACING   Horses are available for hire at beaches and hotels, and stables usually offer lessons and escorted rides. Some horse farms, such as the Baraket Stud Farm at Ghardimaou, near the Algerian border, offer treks for small groups. For those who like to gamble, there are horse races every Sunday at the Ksar Said and Monastir racecourses.

SHOPPING

Throughout Tunisia there are *souks*, or bazaars. The more remote the area, the more important market day is, because it provides an opportunity for social gathering. In the countryside the souks are held in open fields and are known by the day on which the market is held—for example, *Souk el Femma* (Friday's souk) or *Souk el Had* (Sunday's souk).

INTERNET LINKS

http://go-eat-do.com/2013/03/thalassotherapy-in-tunisia-a-spa-treatment-with-french-origins
This is a look at seawater spas in Tunisia.

https://www.gonomad.com/2081-traveling-tunisia-exotic-souks-ancient-ruins-and-fabulous-food
As seen through the eyes of a tourist, this is an overview of Tunisian activities and attractions.

http://www.tunisia-live.net/2012/04/06/lose-yourself-in-the-souks-of-the-tunis-medina
This article explores the souks of the old walled city in Tunis.

FESTIVALS

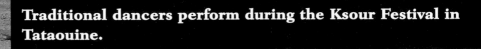

Traditional dancers perform during the Ksour Festival in Tataouine.

LIKE MOST COUNTRIES, TUNISIA celebrates both religious and secular holidays, including national observances. Being a Muslim country, Tunisia follows the annual pattern of Islamic feast days, which occur on different dates each year, according to the Islamic lunar calendar.

The country's secular holidays were created after independence, in an attempt to broaden the nation's identity beyond the purely religious. Those celebrations are state-organized and are accompanied by speeches and parades. Being political in nature, they tend to go in and out of favour as administrations change. For example, former president Zine El Abidine Ben Ali had instituted a holiday to mark the beginning of his presidency, called New Era Day, on November 7, but that is no longer observed. In its place, a new day, Revolution and Youth Day, January 14, celebrates his ouster!

SECULAR AND STATE HOLIDAYS

These special days include New Year's Day, Revolution and Youth Day on January 14; Independence Day, March 20; Martyrs' Day, April 9; Republic Day, July 25; Women's and Family Day, August 13; and Evacuation Day on October 15.

12

The Sahara International Festival in Douz, in the south of Tunisia, is a celebration of the old nomadic way of life in the desert. Some of the popular attractions include camel racing, greyhound racing, traditional dancing, reenacted battles, and a desert-style rodeo.

Patriotic Tunisians wave flags on Revolution and Youth Day in January 2017.

REVOLUTION AND YOUTH DAY   January 14, is a public holiday adopted after the Tunisian Revolution of 2010—2011. When, after four weeks of social and political unrest, President Ben Ali, fled the country, this new holiday was created to commemorate the actions of the protestors, the majority of whom were young people.

MARTYR'S DAY   commemorates the events of April 9, 1938, when a demonstration against the arrest of a popular leader of the Neo-Destour Party ended in violence. The French occupying police force fired on demonstrators, killing at least 22 people and wounding 150 others.

REPUBLIC DAY   on July 25 celebrates the abolition of the monarchy by the National Assembly, resulting in the proclamation of the Republic of Tunisia in 1956. Habib Bourguiba was chosen to be the first President of Tunisia.

WOMEN'S AND FAMILY DAY began as a recognition of women's rights as established in the Code of Personal Status (CPS) in 1956. The holiday has since expanded to include a celebration of the family.

EVACUATION DAY October 15, commemorates the day the last French soldier left the country following the Battle of Bizerte. After the 2011 revolution, Tunisian authorities revived the celebration of this historic date by making it a national holiday.

ISLAMIC HOLIDAYS

Islamic feast days are very much a family celebration, with some festivities spilling out onto the streets as people prepare for the holiday or socialize. The dates of Islamic holidays vary from year to year; the exact dates are calculated after the religious leaders have sighted the new moon. Four major Islamic holidays include Muharram (the Islamic New Year), Eid (EED) al-Fitr, Eid al-Adha, and Mawlid an-Nabi.

EID AL-FITR Eid al-Fitr, the first day of the month of Shawwal, celebrates the end of fasting and self-denial during the month of Ramadan. The day begins solemnly with prayer at the mosque, followed by a visit to the cemetery. Then festivities follow as families enjoy specially prepared food and wear new clothes. Gifts of money are given to children and newly married daughters. Gifts of food are given to the poor to break the fast and enjoy the celebration.

EID AL-ADHA This major festival is celebrated on the tenth day of Dhu al-Hijja, the twelfth month in the Islamic calendar, and commemorates Abraham's willingness to sacrifice his son at God's command. The Qur'an stipulates that able heads of households purchase a sheep for sacrifice and share the meat of the animal with others—one-third to the poor, one-third to friends and neighbors, and one-third to the family. This time of thanksgiving and charity is also an occasion for a family reunion.

THE ISLAMIC CALENDAR

The Islamic era begins with Muhammad's flight from Mecca to Medina in 622 CE. This journey is known as the Hegira, so dates are preceded by AH, or Anno Hegirae, ("year of the Hegira"), rather than AD, meaning anno Domini *("in the year of the Lord") in Latin, or CE, as used in this book, designating "Common Era," which, like* anno Domini, *begins on the year of Christ's birth). Because it is based on the lunar calendar, which has twelve months but only 354 days, the Islamic year is generally about eleven days shorter than the Gregorian year. The twelve months of the Islamic calendar are:*

1. *Muharram*
2. *Safar*
3. *Rabi' al-awwal*
4. *Rabi' al-thani*
5. *Jumada al-awwal*
6. *Jumada al-thani*
7. *Rajab*
8. *Sha'aban*
9. *Ramadan*
10. *Shawwal*
11. *Dhu al-Qi'dah*
12. *Dhu al-Hijja*

The most sacred celebration takes place in Saudi Arabia in the small village of Mina, 4 miles (6.4 km) east of Mecca, where many thousands of Muslims take part in this sacrifice that marks the end of the hajj.

MAWLID AN-NABI Also known as the Prophet Muhammad's birthday, it is celebrated on the twelfth day of Rabi' al-awwal, the third month in the Islamic calendar. It was not observed until the ninth century of Islam, when its exact date was determined. On this day of special prayer, men journey to the main mosque to hear stories of Muhammad's life told by the imam, or religious leader. Women usually gather at a friend's home for their own prayers. The festival is also celebrated with fireworks in Tunisia.

LOCAL AND INTERNATIONAL FESTIVALS

Towns celebrate their own festivals. Some of these include the Orange Festival in Nabeul; the International Festival of Malouf Music in Testour; the Coral Festival in Tabarka; the International Festival of Sousse; the International Festival of Dougga, which features French classical theatre; the folklore festivals in Tozeur, Kerkenna, and the Djerba Islands; the theater and poetry festival in Monastir, and the Sahara Festival in Douz. The Carthage International Cultural Festival is staged in a restored Roman theater where movies, dance, theater, and music are offered, mostly in French.

El Haouaria, on the tip of Cape Bon, is a little village with a passion for falconry. At the falconry festival in June, when the village comes alive with concerts and dances, the falconers display their skills. Falconers train birds to hunt partridge and quail. The best hunters have mammoth appetites and speedy digestion. Trainers control the birds through affection and food.

The Tamerza Festival brings together the Berber communities. Held in April and May, this festival has exhibitions of ancient Berber arts and traditions, folk concerts, parades, theatrical performances, and horse displays.

INTERNET LINKS

http://www.huffingtonpost.co.uk/rupert-parker/planet-appetite-sahara-fetsival-tunisia_b_2395017.html
This article about the Sahara Festival includes many colorful photos.

https://www.timeanddate.com/holidays/tunisia
This site lists Tunisia' holiday calendar by year, with links to explanations of certain days.

http://www.tourismtunisia.com/festivals-in-tunisia
This site lists the local and international festivals held in Tunisia.

FOOD

A sack of chili peppers, essential for making harissa, is on display in a Tunisian market.

13

FRENCH, ITALIAN, ARABIC, Mediterranean, North African, and Middle Eastern flavors and techniques all come together in Tunisian cuisine. Common ingredients include olive oil; honey; spices such as cumin, fennel, ginger, anise, and cinnamon; rice; chickpeas; couscous; seafood; and chicken or lamb. Fruits and vegetables are typically the produce that grows best in the warm, sunny climate—citrus fruits, figs, dates, apricots, and pomegranates, and bell peppers, chili peppers, onions, cucumbers, tomatoes, and eggplants.

Tunisian dishes are often made with *harissa* (ha-REE-sa), a spicy paste made of ground dried chilies, spices, garlic, and olive oil; it is also a popular condiment served alongside many Tunisian dishes.

The best food in Tunisia is found at the sides of streets, where a great variety of freshly made food is sold. Open-air food stalls, cabins, and caravans sell Tunisian fast food—sandwiches filled with tuna, hard-boiled egg, peppers, tomatoes, and onions, dressed with olive oil and

Tunisia is a Muslim country, so the people are forbidden to drink alcoholic beverages. Therefore, the most popular drinks are tea, coffee, and freshly squeezed fruit juices. A citrusy combination of orange, lemon, and grapefruit juice is especially popular in summer.

Shakshuka, or eggs baked in a spicy tomato sauce, is a favorite across Northern Africa.

some harissa sauce. These fast-food places are found near bus stops, railway stations, and markets. The food is cheap and tasty, but customers cannot linger over a meal; they are expected to eat and leave.

FAVORITE TUNISIAN DISHES

A deep-fried savory pastry dish called *brik* (BREEK) usually has a runny egg inside. Other fillings include spicy potato, prawns, anchovies, spinach, and tuna. It is eaten by hand, often dipped in harissa.

Shakshuka (shahk-SHOO-ka) is a spicy vegetable stew of tomatoes, onions, and pimentos (grilled sweet red peppers) with an egg on top. *Chorba* (SHOHR-ba) means "soup."

Chorba Tunisienne is a soup with tomatoes, onions, harissa, and pasta. Fresh *chorba de poisson* (fish soup) is a favorite. Fish is usually served grilled with olive oil and lemon juice; it may also be fried, baked, or stuffed. Fresh seafood is often served with a grilled salad of sweet red peppers, tomatoes, onions, and garlic.

Couscous, the national dish of Tunisia, is served for lunch and dinner. It is made by partially baking semolina flour with water, then grinding it into a fine grain. This is followed by steaming and oiling to separate the grains. Spices added to couscous vary by region, from cinnamon to dried and crushed rosebuds. Couscous is eaten with vegetables and meat ladled on top—perhaps *kafteji* (kahf-TAH-ji), spicy meatballs garnished with chopped liver, onions, peppers, and zucchini, or *kamounia* (kah-MOO-ni-ah), a meat stew flavored with cumin.

A bowl of uncooked couscous.

Maarcassin (mahr-KAH-sin)—wild boar served with a dark sauce—is commonly eaten during winter hunting season. Eating pork and drinking wine may offend others in this predominantly Islamic country, so in restaurants a screen is put up to mask this activity from those who might object.

Ojja (OH-sjah) are eggs scrambled with onions, peppers, tomatoes, and slices of spicy sausage.

Tajine (tah-JEEN), a cake made of eggs and chopped meat, seasoned with parsley, cheese, or pimentos, is something like an Italian frittata or a crustless French quiche. It is best eaten hot, but can be served as cold slices with sauce on top.

DESSERTS

Tunisian baklava, like the Greek version of the sweet dish, has layers of pastry filled with nuts and soaked in honey. Another common sweet is *Makrud* (mahk-ROOD), a semolina cake soaked in honey with dates in the center. *Bouza* (BOO-za) is a dessert of hazelnut or sorghum cream with grilled sesame seeds. *Assida* (ah-SEH-da) is a thick flour cream with grilled pine seeds, but pistachio, hazelnut, and pine kernels can be used as well.

DRINKS

Freshly squeezed fruit juices are the most popular drinks in Tunisia. Orange and lemon juice is especially popular in summer. In Tunisian homes one can also find huge containers full of homemade carrot juice and the triple concoction of orange, lemon, and grapefruit.

Tea is so much a part of the Tunisian lifestyle that wherever two or three Tunisians gather there must be a beaten old pot brewing tea over a charcoal fire. Tea is served strong; sometimes people discard the teaspoon and choose instead to bite on chunks of sugar, and then strain the tea through the sugar in their mouth. Coffee is served Turkish style—cooked fresh in small pots and served strong and black with the grounds in the cup. While waiting for the grounds to settle Tunisians engage in conversation. Tunisian coffee is sometimes flavored with cardamom.

Coffee is served in a café in Tunis.

SNACK FOOD

Unlike in most countries, it is still not very common to see international fast-food restaurants such as McDonald's or Starbucks. People mainly eat local snacks, such as *brik*. This consists of a pastry parcel filled with different fillings such as minced lamb, beef, or vegetables. An egg is cracked over the contents and the pastry folded and deep-fried in oil. *Cassecroute* (cah-she-KROOT)—French bread spread with harissa and filled with olives and vegetables and either tuna, sausage, or egg—is also very popular. Sandwiches tend to be made with local ingredients, such as cream cheese, harissa, tuna, olives, and chili peppers. Tunisians like to eat sweet snacks. Tunisian sweets are usually pastries made with nutty centers, such as pistachios, and drenched in honey or syrup.

A pastry shop displays piles of baked sweets in Sousse.

INTERNET LINKS

http://www.tourismtunisia.com/dishes-that-are-home-to-tunisia
This site presents some photos of popular Tunisian food, but no recipes.

http://www.tunisia-live.net/2011/09/01/our-guide-to-tunisian-cuisine
This is another quick overview of Tunisian cuisine.

TUNISIAN VEGETABLE COUSCOUS

This dish can be a main course in itself or can be served with grilled chicken or lamb kabobs.

3 tablespoons olive oil

1 onion, coarsely chopped

1½ tsp. cumin

1 ½ tsp. cinnamon

1 ½ tsp. paprika

1 tsp. salt

½ tsp. cayenne

2 cloves garlic, minced

1 each zucchini and yellow squash, cut into ½-inch (1.5 cm), half-round slices

1 each red and yellow bell peppers, cored, seeded, and cut into chunks

2 medium carrots, peeled, halved the long way (quartered at thick end), and cut into 3-inch (7.5 cm) pieces

1 14.5-oz (411 g) can chopped tomatoes in juice

Water if needed

1 15.5-oz can (439 g) chickpeas (garbanzos), rinsed and drained

Salt and pepper to taste

1 10-oz package (283 g) plain couscous (not pearled or Israeli-style)

2 cups (475 mL) chicken or vegetable broth

½ cup (75 g) golden raisins

Harissa

In a Dutch oven, warm oil over medium-low heat and lightly sauté the onions and zucchini until just barely soft. Stir in the spices and garlic. Add the peppers and carrots. Add the tomatoes and their juices. Add water if necessary to cover vegetables. Cover the pan and cook until all vegetables are tender but still firm, about 5 minutes. Add the chickpeas. Add salt and pepper to taste.

Meanwhile, prepare couscous according to package directions (use standard stovetop preparation, not microwave), using broth in place of water. Add raisins and cover pot. Let mixture sit 5 to 7 minutes, then fluff with a fork.

To serve, mound couscous in the center of a large shallow bowl or platter and surround with the vegetables. Serve with a small bowl of harissa on the side if desired.

Serves 6

KABER EL LOUZ (TUNISIAN ALMOND BALLS)

These sweet treats are popular for holidays and special occasions.

1 cup (200 g) granulated sugar
¼ tsp kosher salt
1 tsp vanilla
6 Tbsp water
1 Tbsp rosewater
2 cups (240 g) almond meal, almond flour, or
    finely ground almonds

Garnish:
Plain or superfine sugar

In a small saucepan, combine sugar, salt and water. Heat to a boil and then reduce heat to medium-low. Cook, whisking occasionally, until all sugar is dissolved, about 10 minutes. Remove from heat and whisk in the vanilla and the rosewater.

Place almond meal in a medium bowl. Use a wooden spoon to slowly stir in syrup. Once dough has come together, knead on work surface lightly dusted with almond meal until smooth.

Roll each piece into a 1-inch (2.5 cm) ball.

On a plate, a few tablespoons of sugar or superfine sugar. Roll each ball in the sugar and place on serving plate.

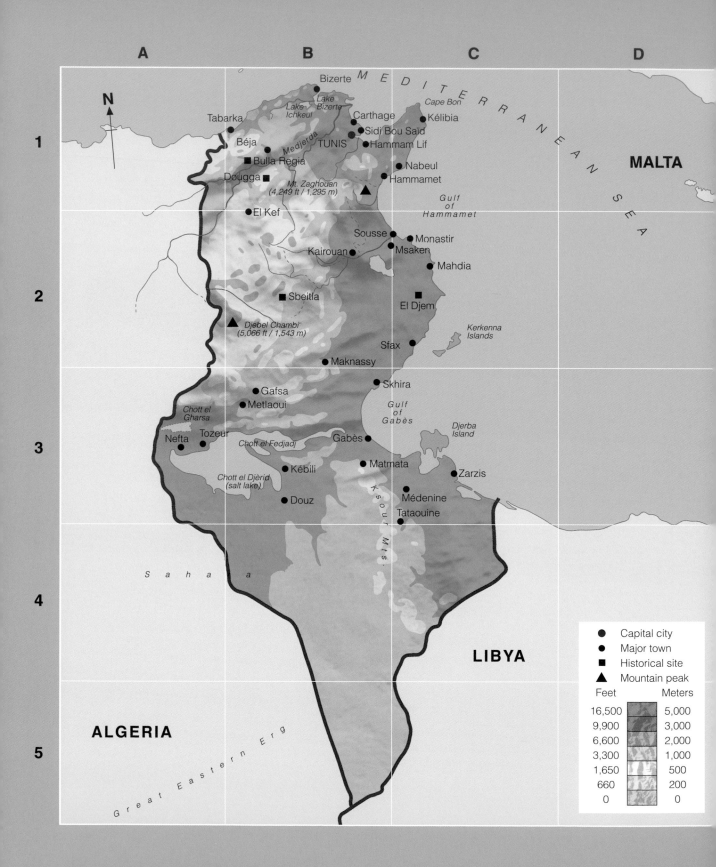

A   B   C   D

MEDITERRANEAN SEA

Bizerte

Lake Ichkeul   *Lake Bizerte*

Tabarka

Cape Bon

Carthage   Kélibia

Béja   Sidi Bou Saïd

Medjerda   TUNIS   Hammam Lif

■ Bulla Regia

Dougga ■   Nabeul

Hammamet

Mt. Zaghouan (4,249 ft / 1,295 m) ▲

● El Kef

Gulf of Hammamet

Sousse ●   Monastir

Kairouan ●   Msaken

Mahdia

■ Sbeitla

El Djem ■

▲ *Djebel Chambi (5,066 ft / 1,543 m)*

Kerkenna Islands

Sfax ●

● Maknassy

● Skhira

Gulf of Gabès

Gafsa ●

● Metlaoui

Chott el Gharsa

Djerba Island

Nefta ●   Tozeur ●

Chott el Fedjadj

Gabès ●

● Kébili

Chott el Djèrid (salt lake)

Matmata ●

Zarzis ●

● Douz

Médenine ●

Tataouine ●

MALTA

S a h a r a

Ksour Mts.

ALGERIA

LIBYA

Great Eastern Erg

	Capital city
●	Capital city
●	Major town
■	Historical site
▲	Mountain peak

Feet	Meters
16,500	5,000
9,900	3,000
6,600	2,000
3,300	1,000
1,650	500
660	200
0	0

N

MAP OF TUNISIA

Algeria,
  A1-A5, B4-B5

Béja, B1
Bizerte, B1
Bulla Regia, B1

Cape Bon, C1
Carthage, B1
Chott el
  Djerid, B3
Chott el
  Fedjadj, B3
Chott el
  Gharsa., A3

Djebel
  Chambi, B2
Djerba
  Island, C3
Dougga, B1
Douz, B3

El Djem, C2
El Kef, B1-B2

Gabes, B3
Gafsa, B3

Great Eastern
  Erg, A5, B4-B5
Gulf of
  Gabes, B3-C3
Gulf of Ham-
  mamet,
  B1-B2, C1-C2

Hammamet, B1
Hammam Lif, B1

Kairouan, B2
Kébili, B3
Kélibia, C1
Kerkenna
  Islands, C2
Ksour
  Mts., B3-B4

Lake Bizerte, B1
Lake Ichkeul, B1
Libya,
  C3-C5, D4-D5

Mahdia, C2
Malta, D1
Maknassy, B2
Matmata, B3

Medenine, C3
Mediterranean
  Sea, A1, B1-B2,
  C1-C3, D1-D3
Medjer-
  da River, B1
Metlaoui, B3
Monastir, C2
Msaken, B2

Nabeul, C1
Nefta, A3

Sahara, A4, B4
Sbeitla, B2
Sfax, C2
Sidi Bou Said, B1
Skhira, B3
Sousse, B2

Tabarka, B1

Tataouine, C3
Tozeur, A3
Tunis, B1

Zag-
  houan, Mt., B1
Zarzis, C3

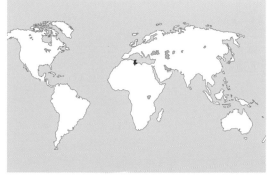

ECONOMIC TUNISIA

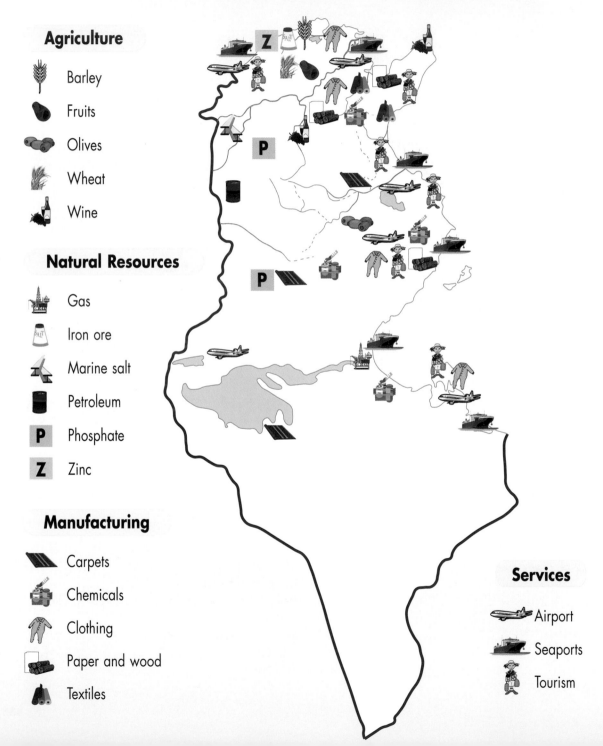

Agriculture

- 🌾 Barley
- 🫒 Fruits
- 🫒 Olives
- 🌾 Wheat
- 🍷 Wine

Natural Resources

- Gas
- Iron ore
- Marine salt
- Petroleum
- **P** Phosphate
- **Z** Zinc

Manufacturing

- Carpets
- Chemicals
- Clothing
- Paper and wood
- Textiles

Services

- ✈ Airport
- 🚢 Seaports
- 🧑 Tourism

ABOUT THE ECONOMY

GROSS DOMESTIC PRODUCT (GDP)(Official Exchange Rate)
$42.39 billion (2016)

GDP PER CAPITA
$11,700 (2016)

GROWTH RATE
1.5 percent (2016)

CURRENCY
Tunisian dinar (TND)
1 US dollar = 2.42 Tunisian dinar (May 2017);
1 dinar = 1,000 milim
Bills: 5, 10, 20, 30, 50 dinar
Coins: 5, 10, 20, 50, 100 milim; ½, 1, 5 dinar

LABOR FORCE
4.038 million (2016)

UNEMPLOYMENT RATE
14 percent (2016)

POPULATION BELOW POVERTY LINE
15.5 percent (2010)

NATURAL RESOURCES
Petroleum, phosphates, iron ore, lead, zinc, salt

AGRICULTURAL PRODUCTS
Olives, olive oil, grain, tomatoes, citrus fruit, sugar beets, dates, almonds; beef, dairy products

INDUSTRIES
petroleum, mining (particularly phosphate, iron ore), tourism, textiles, footwear, agribusiness, beverages

TRADE

Exports:
clothing, semi-finished goods and textiles, agricultural products, mechanical goods, phosphates and chemicals, hydrocarbons, electrical equipment

Trade Partners:
France 30.7 percent, Italy 19.3 percent, Germany 11 percent, Spain 5.2 percent, Algeria 4.2 percent, Libya 4 percent (2015)

Imports:
textiles, machinery and equipment, hydrocarbons, chemicals, foodstuffs

Trade Partners:
France 18.2 percent, Italy 15.2 percent, China 8.5 percent, Germany 7.5 percent, Spain 4.3 percent, Russia 4.1 percent, Algeria 4.1 percent (2015)

TELECOMMUNICATIONS
Telephone fixed lines: 943,508
Mobile cellular phones: 14.598 million (2015)
Internet users: 5.355 million, 48.5 percent (2015)

CULTURAL TUNISIA

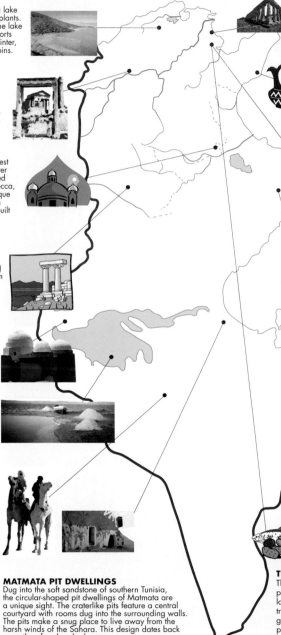

LAKE ICHKEUL
The 23-square-mile (60-square-km) lake is a thriving habitat for birds and plants. Slightly salty and without a tide, the lake has a special ecosystem that supports birds migrating from Europe for winter, as well as frogs, toads, and terrapins.

DOUGGA
Dougga is the site of some of the most beautiful Roman monuments in North Africa, including the Libyco-Punic Mausoleum and the large and impressive temple of the Capitol, both of which date from the second century BCE.

GREAT MOSQUE OF KAIROUAN
The Great Mosque of Kairouan is the oldest and most important Muslim place of prayer in North Africa and is commonly regarded as the fourth-holiest site in Islam (after Mecca, Medina, and Jerusalem). The Great Mosque dates from 863 CE. The massive wooden doors leading into the prayer hall were built in 1829 and are beautifully carved.

SUFETULA, SBEITLA
The Roman ruins of Sufetula contain the best-preserved forum temple (a style of temple—usually used as a meeting place) in Tunisia. Dating from 139 CE, the forum was the center of the town in Roman times, and has survived nearly nineteen centuries with little damage.

NEFTA
Myths tell of Nefta first being settled by Noah's grandson, Kostel, as a place where "the waters first boiled" after landing from the Flood. An important religious town, Nefta is home to Tunisia's Sufi sect. There are more than twenty Sufi mosques in the town, as well as many holy shrines.

CHOTT EL JERID
Tunisia has many desert salt lakes, and Chott el Jerid is the largest. The lake is completely dry for nine months of the year, though it does flood after rainfall. It is sometimes known as the Lake of Marks because of the palm trunks that were planted across the lake for traveling caravans to use as markers.

FESTIVAL OF SAHARA, DOUZ
Held each winter at the end of December, the Festival of the Sahara celebrates the life and culture of the great desert. Highlights of the festival include camel racing, sand hockey, pottery, music, and traditional marriage customs.

MATMATA PIT DWELLINGS
Dug into the soft sandstone of southern Tunisia, the circular-shaped pit dwellings of Matmata are a unique sight. The craterlike pits feature a central courtyard with rooms dug into the surrounding walls. The pits make a snug place to live away from the harsh winds of the Sahara. This design dates back more than four hundred years.

CARTHAGE
The remains of the ancient city of Carthage are shrouded in myth and romance. Today a series of widely spaced ruins is all that is left of the port city that once competed with Rome for power in the Mediterranean.

NABEUL POTTERY AND STONE CARVING
The town of Nabeul is home to Tunisia's ancient and thriving pottery industry. Along with Djerba, Nabeul is the national center for arts and crafts. Nabeul is also a center for stone carving, and many buildings and hotels in the town display impressive stone doorways, columns, and facades.

BARDO MUSEUM, TUNIS
Situated in the Bardo Palace, the Bardo Museum holds the best collection of Tunisian artifacts in the country. Colorful mosaics from the Carthaginian, Roman, and Byzantine periods form the center of the collection, including a massive mosaic portrait of the Latin poet Virgil (1,475 square feet/137 square m), which is believed to be the largest mosaic portrait in existence.

EL JEM'S AMPHITHEATER
The remains of the Roman amphitheater in El Jem date from the third century BCE and is a designated World Heritage site. This huge, well-preserved construction could hold up to thirty thousand spectators, making it possibly the third or fourth biggest amphitheater in the Roman Empire.

THE SOUK OF THE MEDINA, TUNIS
The old district of Tunis is home to numerous mosques, palaces, mausoleums, and fountains, as well as the largest and busiest souk (market) in the country. Here traders will bargain for all kinds of North African goods, including clothing, rugs, animals, street food, pottery, mosaics, and perfume.

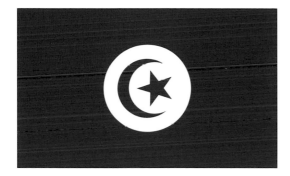

OFFICIAL NAME
Tunisian Republic

NATIONAL FLAG
Red with a white disk in the center bearing a red crescent nearly encircling a red five-pointed star; the crescent and star are traditional symbols of Islam.

NATIONALITY
Tunisian

CAPITAL
Tunis

POPULATION
11,134,588 (2016)

LANGUAGES
Arabic (official and one of the languages of commerce); French (no official status, but plays a major role in the country and is spoken by about two-thirds of the population); Berber (Tamazight)

ETHNIC GROUPS
Arab 98 percent, European 1 percent, Jewish and other 1 percent

RELIGIONS
Muslim (mostly Sunni) 99.1 percent, other (includes Christian, Jewish, Shia Muslim, and Baha'i), 1 percent

LIFE EXPECTANCY AT BIRTH
Total population: 76.1 years
Male: 74 years
Female: 78.4 years (2016)

INFANT MORTALITY RATE
21.6 deaths/1,000 live births

LITERACY RATE
81.8 percent
Male: 89.6 percent
Female: 74.2 percent (2015)

TIMELINE

IN TUNISIA	IN THE WORLD
circa 1100 BCE • Phoenicians settle on the North African coast. 814 BCE • The city of Carthage is founded.	• 753 BCE Rome is founded.
600s CE • Arabs conquer Tunisia. 909 • Berbers capture the region from the Arabs.	• 1000 CE The Chinese invent gunpowder. • 1100 Rise of the Incan civilization in Peru
1044 • The Zirid Dynasty becomes the first native Tunisian group to govern the country.	• 1206 Genghis Khan unifies the Mongols and starts conquest of the world.
1518 • Algiers and Tunis, Barbary pirate states in North Africa, are founded. 1574 • Tunis becomes a regency of the Ottoman Empire.	• 1492 Christopher Columbus sails to the Americas. • 1558–1603 Reign of Elizabeth I of England
	• 1789–1799 The French Revolution
1881 • French troops occupy Tunis and Tunisia becomes a French protectorate.	• 1869 The Suez Canal is opened.
1956 • Tunisia becomes independent, with Habib Bourguiba as prime minister. 1957 • Tunisia becomes a republic.	• 1914–1919 World War I • 1939–1945 World War II

IN TUNISIA	IN THE WORLD
1963 • The French evacuate Bizerta, their last base.	• 1969 Neil Armstrong becomes the first person to walk on the moon.
1975 • The constituent assembly appoints Bourguiba president for life.	
1981 • The first multiparty parliamentary elections are held since independence. President Bourguiba's party wins a landslide victory.	
	• 1986 Nuclear power disaster at Chernobyl in Ukraine
1987 • Prime Minister Zine El Abidine Ben Ali takes power.	
1989 • Ben Ali wins presidential election.	• 1991 Breakup of the Soviet Union
1999 • First multiparty presidential elections; Ben Ali wins a third term.	
2000 • Habib Bourguiba dies at age 96.	• 2001 Terrorists attack United States on September 11. • 2003 War in Iraq begins.
2004 • President Ben Ali wins a fourth term.	
2011 • Tunisian Revolution sparks Arab Spring; ousts Ben Ali.	• 2008 US elects first African American president, Barack Obama.
2014 • New constitution is approved; Beji Caid Essebsi becomes president.	
2015 • Terrorist attacks in Bardo Museum and Sousse.	• 2015–2016 ISIS launches terror attacks in Belgium and France.
2017 • Prime Minister Youssef Chahed announces fight against corruption.	• 2017 Donald Trump becomes US president. Britain begins Brexit process of leaving the EU.

GLOSSARY

baraka (BAH-ra-kah)
Spiritual powers.

Berbers
Indigenous people of North Africa.

bey
Ruler of Tunis, the title adopted by the monarch of Tunisia. The monarchy was made obsolete in 1957, after Tunisia became independent.

brik (BREEK)
Tunisian snack.

Cassecroute (cah-she-KROOT)
French bread spread with harrissa and filled with olives, vegetables, and either tuna, sausage, or egg.

chott (SHOT)
Salt lake. Sometimes spelt shott or shatt.

Djebel
Hill or mountain.

Eid (EED)
Festival. Two major Islamic festivals in Tunisia are Eid al-Fitr and Eid al-Adha.

ghorfa (GHOR-fa)
Arabic for "room;" a storage area for grain.

harissa (ha-REE-sa)
Paste of chilies, garlic, spices, and olive oil used in Tunisian cooking.

Ifriqiya
Arabic name for the region of Tunisia, the area of which changed frequently throughout history.

ksar (SAHR)
Arabic for "fortress;" a fortified granary.

Maghreb
North African Arab states, including Morocco, Algeria, Tunisia, and sometimes Libya.

marabouts
people who possess spiritual powers; saints

medina
Old section of cities, usually featuring narrow alleys lined with houses, shops, and mosques.

ribat(ri-BAHT)
Fortress built by Muslim rulers.

Sahel
Shore or coast; the Sahel refers to the coastal region in eastern Tunisia.

sidi (see-DI)
"Master," title of respect reserved for holy men.

souk
Bazaar or open-air market.

zaouia (zo-EE-ya)
Center of a religious brotherhood such as that of the Sufi sect of Islam.

FOR FURTHER INFORMATION

BOOKS

Fraihat, Ibrahim. *Unfinished Revolutions: Yemen, Libya, and Tunisia after the Arab Spring.* New Haven: Yale University Press, 2016.

Tunisia (Eyewitness Travel Guides). London: DK Publishing, 2011.

Willis, Michael. *Politics and Power in the Maghreb: Algeria, Tunisia and Morocco from Independence to the Arab Spring.* New York: Oxford University Press, 2014.

WEBSITES

Al Jazeera. Tunisia news archives. http://www.aljazeera.com/topics/country/tunisia.html

BBC News. Tunisia country profile. http://www.bbc.com/news/world-africa-14107241

CIA World Factbook, Tunisia. https://www.cia.gov/library/publications/the-world-factbook/geos/ts.html

Lonely Planet. Tunisia. https://www.lonelyplanet.com/tunisia

The Guardian. Tunisia news archives. https://www.theguardian.com/world/tunisia

The New York Times. Tunisia news archives. https://www.nytimes.com/topic/destination/tunisia

Tunisian National Tourist Office. http://www.discovertunisia.com/en

BIBLIOGRAPHY

Al Jazeera. "Pollution in Gabes, Tunisia's shore of death." June 14, 2013. http://www.aljazeera.com/indepth/features/2013/06/20136913247297963.html

BBC News. Tunisia country profile. http://www.bbc.com/news/world-africa-14107241

Blaise, Lilia. "Self-Immolation, Catalyst of the Arab Spring, Is Now a Grim Trend." *The New York Times*, July 9, 2017. https://www.nytimes.com/2017/07/09/world/africa/self-immolation-catalyst-of-the-arab-spring-is-now-a-grim-trend.html

CIA World Factbook. Tunisia. https://www.cia.gov/library/publications/the-world-factbook/geos/ts.html

Constituteproject.org. Tunisia's Constitution of 2014. https://www.constituteproject.org/constitution/Tunisia_2014.pdf

Freedom House. Freedom in the World 2017: Tunisia profile. https://freedomhouse.org/report/freedom-world/2017/tunisia

Gall, Carlotta. "Corruption Crackdown Intensifies in Tunisia, and the People Cheer." *The New York Times*, June 25, 2017. https://www.nytimes.com/2017/06/25/world/africa/corruption-crackdown-intensifies-in-tunisia-and-the-people-cheer.html

Kabbani, Shaykh Muhammad Hisham. "Understanding Islamic Law." The Islamic Supreme Council of America. http://islamicsupremecouncil.org/understanding-islam/legal-rulings/52-understanding-islamic-law.html

Lageman, Thessa. "Horror still fresh a year after Tunisia museum attack." Al Jazeera, March 18, 2016. http://www.aljazeera.com/news/2016/03/horror-fresh-year-tunisia-museum-attack-160314115053039.html

Middle East Eye. "Tunisia jails four men for eating in public during Ramadan." June 1, 2017. http://www.middleeasteye.net/news/tunisia-jails-four-men-breaking-ramadan-fasting-rules-673557648

Reuters. "Tunisia sees 30 percent tourism growth in 2017." Reuters, March 21, 2017. http://www.reuters.com/article/us-tunisia-economy-tourism-idUSKBN16S1K1

Ryan, Yasmine. "The tragic life of a street vendor." Al Jazeera, January 20, 2011. http://www.aljazeera.com/indepth/features/2011/01/201111684242518839.html

——————— "How Tunisia's revolution began." Al Jazeera, January 26, 2011. http://www.aljazeera.com/indepth/features/2011/01/2011126121815985483.html

"Tethered by history." *The Economist*, August 14, 2014. http://www.economist.com/news/briefing/21606286-failures-arab-spring-were-long-time-making-tethered-history

Tunisia Live Team. "Climate Change: The Threat No One's Talking About." Tunisia Live, December 5, 2015. http://www.tunisia-live.net/2015/12/05/environment

Wismayer, Henry. "The Terror Attack That Destroyed Tunisia's Tourist Industry." Vice, August 4, 2016. https://www.vice.com/en_us/article/8genja/tunisia-tourist-industry-terror-attack

INDEX

INDEX